D1469943

TOKENS
OF
MYSELF

Also by Celestine Sibley

Turned Funny
For All Seasons
Children, My Children
The Magic Realm of Sallie Middleton
Jincey
Small Blessings
Young'uns
Mothers Are Always Special
Day by Day
Especially at Christmas
Sweet Apple Gardening Book
A Place Called Sweet Apple
Dear Store
Christmas in Georgia
Peachtree Street USA—An Affectionate Portrait of Atlanta
The Malignant Heart

Celestine Sibley

TOKENS
OF
MYSELF

LONGSTREET PRESS
Atlanta, Georgia

Published by
LONGSTREET PRESS
2150 Newmarket Parkway
Suite 102
Marietta, Georgia 30067

Printed in the United States of America

1st printing, 1990

Library of Congress Catalog Card Number: 90-061852

ISBN 929264-40-1

This book was printed by R. R. Donnelley & Sons, Harrisonburg, Virginia. The text was set in Bembo by Typo-Repro Service, Inc., Atlanta, Georgia. Cover design by Paulette Livers-Lambert. Text design by Jill Dible.

For readers of patience, tolerance, and good will.
Bless you for sustaining me all these years.

Contents

Foreword

A bred-in-the-bone newspaper reporter hasn't much respect for a columnist. There he (or she) sits spinning improbabilities out of his (or her) mid-section, serving up opinions, turning out what my long-time office roommate Harold Martin called "thumb-suckers." And all the while the rest of us, anonymous foot soldiers, are out there where the news is happening, grappling with facts instead of feelings, getting blisters on our feet and sometimes knots on our heads. Column-writing—bah, an occupation for sissies!

Or so I thought in all the years I was a practicing reporter. I liked going to fires and floods and murders and political rallies. I liked the plain, stripped down, no-maybe's prose that was our style.

And then one day in the 1940's I had to take some time off from going to murder trials, the police station, Grady hospital and pinch-hitting at the city hall and the capitol, to go get my children's tonsils out. I went in to see our editor Ralph McGill. Everybody went in to see Mr. McGill in those days. The old flower man at the corner, the punchy newspaper street salesman, who courted a woman across Marietta Street by barking like a dog, strippers like Gipsy Rose Lee, ballet dancers, drunks and statesmen. They all dropped in on our boss—and so did reporters whose rent was overdue or whose kinfolks were in jail. Mr. McGill was so relieved that I didn't want anything special except a little time that he said cordially, "You don't have to take time off. Write a column."

"Aw, I couldn't do that!" I said. I didn't add that I didn't even like columns, except, of course, his.

"Sure you can," he said. "You're getting your children's tonsils out. Everybody has to do that. Write about it."

Everybody did indeed haul their children in for tonsilectomies in those days but from the standpoint of newsworthiness I thought it was puny stuff. I did it, of course, and the next one about Miss Rose Mae Ashby's plants in old chamber pots in front of a decaying mansion on Pulliam Street.

From that day forward I was a sometimes, off-and-on columnist, turning out three to six a week from wherever I was when I had written "30" to the news stories of the day. Columns, at least my columns, were always secondary to the news. The story I was sent to cover came first and after that I was free to write the not terribly significant, never penetrating, things which interested me perhaps more than the vital issues aimed at Page One.

But it wasn't capricious play work because Mr. McGill told me at the start that if you signed on to write a column you didn't miss. Come illness, family crisis, vacation, even death, you got that column in. Space had been reserved for it. In my case space was in different places through the years — on the editorial page, on what we call Op Ed for opposite editorial page, in what was then the women's section and for a time "running wild," the makeup editor's quixotic word for stuff he had to stick in somewhere.

Mr. McGill himself didn't miss. During the final illness of his first wife, May Elizabeth, he sat by her hospital bed twenty-four hours a day and wrote his column in longhand. With that example I have written on portable typewriters in the back of staff cars on the way from tornadoes, tobacco markets, trials. I have balanced my typewriter on my stomach and written from a hospital bed, kept Rock Hudson waiting while I phoned the office from a Hollywood studio commissary, hauled the phone into a candidate for governor's hotel bathroom while election returns were being tabulated in the other room. It wasn't that I presumed I had anything important or earth-shaking to write but I had been told not to miss and I have only rarely.

Mr. McGill was right to steer me to write about everyday, commonplace experiences of ordinary people. The mail told me that then and it continues to say the same now, roughtly 10,000 columns later.

Harold Martin, a lyrical columnist for us and a contributing editor for the *Saturday Evening Post,* put it another way.

"When you write about your children," he said, "you are writing about everybody's children. The only excuse for a personal column is that if you are lucky you touch universal experience."

Oddly enough, I began to LIKE writing a column. It sharpened my attention. A news story, for which I have the greatest respect, might not have room for feelings, for the smell of dust and floor oil in a courtroom, for the hound dogs in the yard and the nursing mother in the front row. You couldn't put the flavor of the church ladies' gingerbread in an account of a murder trial but it was there, part of the experience of Big Court in a little mountain town. With a column to write you could add a dimension to the news.

For instance, there was no place in the coverage of the famous Coweta County murder trial of many years ago to describe the primitive log cabin home of the self-styled "seer and oracle" Miss Mayhayley Lancaster, who was a key witness in the case against the landlord-defendant John Wallace. In a column I could make a visit to her house a personal adventure and relate that her sister, Miss Sallie, claimed to have been so ill she couldn't keep a thing but parched corn and whiskey on her stomach. I could tell how Miss Mayhayley herself went to sleep while telling my fortune.

It wasn't news but it was something I loved about covering the news. It was touching people where they were and writing about it.

To me covering straight news is still the primary function of a newspaper and the highest calling of those of us who proudly call ourselves reporters. But you get something extra, something powerfully moving and exciting, when you write a column. Newspaper readers are no longer faceless, nameless people with a quarter to spend. They are people who call you up and write you letters and sometimes send you photographs of their gardens or their babies. What you write is often very personal, painfully personal. And what you get back is also personal, the griefs, the triumphs, the humor of people who trust you to read what they write and to understand.

The columns in this book are an editor's choice from the years' accumulation. I didn't pick them. I wouldn't know how. But I am touched that Chuck Perry and his staff thought them worth assembling and passing on. It makes me glad that forty-odd years ago Ralph McGill said, "Celestine, write a column."

Home
&
Hearth

*T*he first fireplace fire of the season should be a time of celebration—a gathering of family and friends, the breaking of bread, the sharing of salt, the singing of songs. But no matter how much Johnny Beckman knows about the weather that's coming, no matter how attentively I listen, how carefully I examine the sky and check the thermometer, the weather always surprises me.

The other morning it was CO-OLD, and there I was barefooted and breezily clad in a skimpy shift. If I went rummaging for a warm robe and woolly slippers I would awaken the rest of the family, and I am selfishly disposed to let sleepers sleep.

The predawn hours are my time of day, a time for quiet and little personal projects. If it's nothing more inspiring than emptying or filling the dishwasher, it's something I like to do alone. Best of all is that first cup of coffee, taken in silence on the back steps with only the dogs and the cat to nag me—and they do.

But it was too cold for the back steps the other morning. Too cold really for the house unless I could find a fire. And that's what I did. I grabbed the first coat—one the boys left behind—I could put a hand to, stuck my feet in my hiking shoes, grabbed a flashlight and went to the woodshed.

It was a lovely fire, paper and fat light'ard followed by one of the logs from our felled apple tree, and it burned green and blue and gold as only fruitwood burns. I sat on the old bench before it got too hot for me, and then I moved back to the rocker and let the old chair's creak complement the whisper and the crackle of the fire.

There are people in this world with grander houses, I conceded, some that don't have leaks in the roof or drafts in the walls. But I felt immeasurably lucky sitting there looking at my fire and feeling its beneficent glow on my face and my feet. If I had to choose between a palace and a fireplace, I believe I'd take the fireplace without hesitation.

One of the boys passed through the living room on the way to the kitchen and returned, coffee cup in hand, to ask that I was doing up so early.

"Sitting here feeling lucky," I said.

"Maybe so," he said, shivering a little and getting closer to the fire.

He clearly didn't want me to expound my theory of personal good fortune, at least not until he had sipped a little coffee to fortify himself for conversation. But I had been up long enough to want to talk about it and I gave him a comprehensive rundown on the fortuitous circumstances which provided that I always have a fireplace.

❧ ❧ ❧

He went away and I was left alone remembering the many fireplaces I have known — the log-burning one in our living room when I was a child, the spare, efficient little one in my bedroom, which could accommodate coal but was equally receptive to mill ends, which we had in bountiful supply, the old yellow tile in our living room on 13th Street, the rock and clay mountain fireplace in our cabin on Holly Creek.

It happened a couple of days later that we drove over to Social Circle to see our longtime friends, Tom and Wylly Folk St. John. Wylly was an ornament to our Sunday magazine for many years before she went home to write highly successful juvenile mysteries. They bought an old house on a pretty street in Social Circle and the first thing I noticed about it after I got past the deep shady porch with its wicker furniture and hanging baskets, was a coal fire in the living room grate.

"I like to have a fire when there are friends to sit beside it," Wylly said. "We have six fireplaces in this house, and they all work."

Talk about a lucky woman.

October 7, 1980

*W*inter nights at Sweet Apple are still pretty quiet despite the presence of new neighbors who have late-returning teen-agers driving motorcycles and sports cars. There are long reaches of silence so deep and unbroken you stand on the back steps and think you might hear the smoke rising from the chimney.

The moon and the stars still dominate the night sky, although they are getting increasing competition from the flush of lights pushing against the horizon from the subdivision down the road. Five years ago you could walk the night roads around Sweet Apple and not see a light of any kind for miles.

And you could lie in bed and listen, hearing nothing but the creaking and stirring an old house makes when winter cold enters its bones, or, maybe on another night, the fox hunters running their dogs from the big rock overlooking the river.

We hated to see the fox hunters take their business elsewhere. The knowledge that they had parked their pickup trucks in a circle, unloaded their dogs and were even then sitting around an oak and hickory fire passing a bottle and listening, was somehow comforting.

🍎 🍎 🍎

We could hear Old Bess and Jimmy Joe and Sweet Lu running sometimes, their bell-like voices lifting on the hillsides, fluting in the hollows. That kind of fox hunting is a restful sport, requiring little of the hunter except a knowledge of his hound's voice and the ability to gauge progress from canine music.

The fox hunters come no more. Maybe we're getting too settled for them. But other dogs run at night, ours among them, and sometimes I pull up the covers and lie very still and listen.

Stranger, the somewhat-sheep dog, who looks like an unmade bed in the daytime, sings tenor at night. Raises his muzzle and bays at the moon, achieving, it sometimes seems to me, pure choirboy tones. His sidekick, Mason, a stocky brindle fellow whose lineage escapes me, has a pleasant baritone which he uses in the hope of cutting short the piercing jeremiad of Stranger. He can howl, hound-like, if he wants to. But the staccato bark is more his style and he offers it to punctuate and mayhap to interrupt Stranger.

Sweet Apple dogs have recently been joined by a female friend who is the size and shape and color of a length of bologna. We don't know her name so we call her

Lady Dog. She is a shy young thing who smiles and wags her tail at us but she has been reluctant to get within petting range. She checks out the feeding pans and if the bill of fare meets with her approval she fastidiously samples it. And then, a little like Miriam Hopkins in "These Three," she lies down under the maple tree between Stranger and Mason — an impartial equidistance from each.

❦ ❦ ❦

Sometimes we don't see Lady Dog for a day or two and we assume that she has returned to her home, wherever that is. But comes the night, we hear her voice.

She has an amazing bass voice, deeper, stronger, louder than the voices of either of her swains. When I hear it coming out of that short-legged, sausage-shaped little female I get the giggles. It's as if Shirley Temple belted out a song with the voice of Ezio Pinza.

So when the moon comes up and the rail fence glitters with a rime of frost, the dogs will be absent from the backyard, you can bet on that. They live by no fixed and immutable schedule but on a moonlight night in November they've places to go and things to serenade.

I wonder about them running through brambles and thickets, stirring up things that may be under logs and rocks, bounding up hills, wading through creeks. But then I hear their voices — the fine tenor of Stranger, the baritone of Mason, the rich bass of Lady Dog — and the weight of the bedcovers seems heavy, the walls of the house close. I'm envying my dogs.

November 26, 1980

*M*y gadfly friend who jeers at my pre-occupation with what she once called my "bucolic, backward and boorish" life at Sweet Apple, has been silent for so long I feared she had taken up living in Grand Central Station as a bag lady. But no, she's still a high-rise, condominium, don't-take-me-away-from-the-streetlights type. I found a letter from her awaiting me when I came home from the beach.

Daylight is arriving later and later these days, she wrote with what I felt to be unseemly pleasure, and she wonders what excuse I have for arising at 4 a.m., "if you don't have the excuse of junketing around in the bushes."

"Or perhaps," she added, "you have become civilized and stay decently in bed until the sun rises?"

It hadn't occurred to me that I needed an excuse for enjoying that alluring time of day when the world is quiet and you don't have to do a darned thing you don't want to do. Nobody is ready for a meal or needing clean clothes or eager for conversation. You can drink your coffee and listen to the silence and read any old thing that strikes your fancy whether it be something that you promised to read or something that you simply bumble into. (How long has it been since you read "The Rime of the Ancient Mariner" or Rupert Brooke's lovely lines, *"If I should die, think only this of me . . ."* or Alan Seeger's *"I have a rendezvous with Death/At some disputed barricade"*?) In the real daytime I might be able to sit in my mother's old rocking chair and read poetry if I want to, but I never have. I think this is due to my upbringing, which held that it was somehow immoral to "read for pleasure" before noon. If there was any conceivable job that needed doing, you were a slothful slob to sit around reading poetry. But at 4 a.m., ah, you can indulge yourself.

There's also that other pursuit which, I'm sure, would send my urban friend into gales of laughter. But the early morning hours are mine for what we country women call "putting by" winter food. Now I have heard all I want to hear from those derisive souls who think it foolish and impractical to can four pints of tomatoes at 4 a.m. They can give you statistics on how much more expensive this is than to buy a few cans as you need them at the supermarket. They know something I have never been able to figure out — how much you squander on cooking gas and electricity. But their four Roma plants aren't spilling beautiful armaranthine fruit all over the ground. These lovely tomatoes I set out late because I had them, but without much hope. If they bore, they would make a splendid base for spaghetti and pizza sauce, being meaty sauce-type tomatoes, rather than the big juicy salad and sandwich variety. Well, they bore . . . all over the place.

Would you leave them sprawling in the grass to be devoured by terrapins and rabbits? I picked them and set them on the meat block where I could admire them for a few hours — the prettiest still life I've ever seen. And the next pre-dawn found me in the basement rooting out pint jars and the big blue granite canner.

The whole ritual of washing and scalding jars, skinning the satiny plum-shaped fruit and sealing it back of glass is a soothing ceremony to me. I like the warmth from the bubbling kettle of water, the kitchen smells, the quiet. And when the sun comes up over the hill behind the big water oak tree, I lift the sealed and processed tomatoes from their water bath and set them on a clean towel on the meat block, ready to call for photographers.

Practical? Perhaps not, but then who asked Titian or Renoir if they had run up their gas bill?

September 22, 1982

*T*here may not be another woman alive who is not glad to have a non-leaking roof over her head. But I must confess that when I got home in the late afternoon and saw reroofing was in progress, I nearly cried. It's not that I am unalterably committed to leaks in the roof, although I probably don't mind them as much as a more civilized person would. But I just hate to see the old roof go.

When I first met Sweet Apple cabin, it wore a rusty tin roof with the pitiful though rakish air of a drunk on a spree. Part of the tin had blown off, exposing white oak shakes that may have been a hundred years old and giving egress to honeysuckle vines, nesting birds and snakes. Rebuilding the roof was a major part of remodeling. The tin and the old "boards," as those who made them call the shingles, were summarily ripped off and hauled away. Down went new rafters, replacing the peeled poles of 1844. Down went plywood decking and insulation and tar paper.

It was time for boards and our dear neighbor, Mr. Lum Crow, then seventy-nine years old, happened to hear of a supply in a buggy house on an abandoned farm up in Pickens County. We tracked down the name and address of the owner, the widow of the man who had rived those boards and stacked them there forty years ago, and we called upon her. She was willing to sell the lot for fifty dollars. I was glad to buy.

🍎 🍎 🍎

One cold frosty Saturday morning, Mr. Crow and a neighbor with a truck, the late Clint Goodwin, and I journeyed north to Pickens County and the old buggy house. It was good work, hauling and stacking the rough fragrant shingles, and I was delighted with Mr. Crow's verdict.

"Them's good boards," he said.

Carpenters, led by Judson Carter and his lieutenant, Tom Vance, a man then in his seventies, were already on the roof when we arrived, and Mr. Crow and I made haste to join them. There were those who thought I wasn't competent to help roof that little cabin, but Mr. Crow, acquainted with generations of "stout and nimble women" in his own family, believed in me. We all worked along together until the sunlight, which had been strong and warming, waned and we could no longer see to line the shingles up straight and true on the lines Judson had set for us.

Then Mr. Crow distributed a sack full of sweet, tart little lady apples and we all stood back and admired our handiwork.

Half that roof still turns the rain, the heat and sometimes sleet and snow. The rest of it is picturesque but inefficient. The old boards curled and turned green, splitting here and there with a kind of gap-toothed leer. A hard rain deposits puddles like coldhearted visitors all over the house.

❦ ❦ ❦

It was time. I knew it was. But I loved that old roof, and where can you find seasoned forty-year-old shakes these days?

For days now they've been working on the roof, ripping off the old shakes with a tearing noise that sounds like a human cry of distress. They have hammered and sawed and thumped around, searching the sky anxiously when a cloud passes over the face of the sun. I climb the ladder to help with such odd womanish jobs as they assign me. It's lovely on the housetop with all those treetops enclosing you in green and the sun hot on your back. But somehow this roofing job hasn't any glamour. Now if we just had some of them "good boards". . . .

October 5, 1982

*T*he children in our family have long derided our inherited wake-up mechanism. My mother called it "setting your mind." She could do it and each of us in turn has found that by determining at bedtime that we would awaken at 4 or 6 or 7 a.m. that we could pull it off. Of course, we might wake up prematurely a few times, checking the clock anxiously, but mostly it works. You set your mind and there you are, awake.

What's the matter with alarm clocks? ask the young. What's the matter with a good clock radio? Or leaving the television set on all night to start its clatter while you are supine and defenseless?

I'll tell you what's wrong with all these artificial aids to beginning a day: They are noisy. If there's any special thing of value about the early morning, it's quiet. Set your mind and it silently nudges you to wakefulness. The room is dark and maybe the windows, too, depending upon the hour you choose, and you can lie there a moment reviewing dreams, sorting out your problems, anticipating the day.

Of course, the best part of it is padding through the dark, silent house and turning on the coffee. It helps if you have set it up the night before so all you have to do is plug it in. But even if you didn't "set" the coffee when you set your mind, it's not a bad chore, drawing fresh water, measuring out the fragrant grounds.

Then there's that little space of time, while you wait. I have a spot I like by the living room window. Log cabins, as I have mentioned here before, are short on windows. Our living room has but two smallish ones. But they are blessedly placed, one on the east, one on the west. I choose the east one and sit beside it waiting for the coffee and watching the light come to a patch of sky over the roof of the adjoining cabin. It is a small segment of sky I watch but very eloquent, changing from darkness to daytime slowly, almost majestically, first black, then gray and then a range of lovely colors. Some days it is rose and gold streaked, some a bright vermillion. Now and then the blueness takes over, clear and unsullied.

The world is very quiet at sunrise. Even whirring, rumbling appliances which constitute the heartbeat of the present-day house, are blessedly drowsing. Only the old Seth Thomas clock on the shelf speaks — a steady measured articulation of the passing moments. (As my clock-repairing friends have all assured me, all that clock needed was a level place to sit. Levelness is in short supply in Sweet Apple cabin. Not on the fireboard, not on any cupboard. We finally achieved it when my grandson Bird hung a little shelf on the wall — a crooked *looking* little shelf which, according to the spirit level, is the only steady and even thing in the house.)

The clock speaks and presently the steaming coffee burbles up in the pot and I get a cup and return to my niche by the window. Now the woods and the yard are coming into focus. The branches of the hackberry tree at the edge of the terrace are still leaf-clothed but not completely. Maple leaves are already making puddles of gold and topaz over the ground. The other trees will follow soon. The rough grass is glistening with dew. Soon it will be frost. Weeds and dead seed pods and drying stalks fill the flower beds, but some things make a last grab at summertime. A tired looking geranium I thought was ready to quit has three new blooms. Sultana plants from last summer's seeds have come up between the bricks of the terrace. A bird comes to the little shell-shaped water container under the peach tree and his mate calls out to him from the rooftop. A squirrel appears from somewhere and begins his before-breakfast gymnastics in the maple tree.

Day has arrived with what seems to me to be a quiet, jangle-free sense of excitement.

October 11, 1982

*I*t rained at Sweet Apple and brought us a little relief from the heat. The sun-crisped old shingles on the roof let in the rainwater but that was all right with me. I stood under a leak and let it fall on my face, grateful for the cool, not minding a bit if it soaked me and all my possessions. With relief on hand I could be more appreciative than I have been of summertime.

The local family and a couple of visitors from afar, including my New Jersey son-in-law, were with us for a summer evening's meal out under the trees. And looking around at them sprawled in deck chairs in the shade of a little grove of maple, chinaberry, dogwood and cherry trees, I felt a great sweeping sense of the Earth's slow turning, the rightness of the time, the goodness of being together.

The meat for supper slowly smoked in the outdoor cooker back beyond the garden. Three little boys chased one another across the yard. A mourning dove sounded down in the woods and presently a timid, sun-warmed breeze stirred around in the leaves overhead.

Summer, the full season, the ripe season, the time of chairs in the yard, July flies sawing away in the trees, lightning bugs winking over the grass, a watermelon cooling in a box of ice under the trees.

The newest baby in the crowd, a three-month-old named Rachel, arrived in her Sunday finery but was speedily stripped to her diaper and passed from hand to hand, lap to lap, smiling and cooing and reaching pink-velvet, starfish-shaped little hands for tinkling glasses.

We spread the picnic cloth and set out the plates, my daughter and I, and paused, salad bowl and iced tea pitcher in hand, to discuss the concerts at Chastain Park. We remember Theatre *Under*, not *Of*, the Stars of years ago and the delight of sitting on a hillside in the darkness and listening to the music. We spoke of swimming and the chilren's progress and the late Freddie Lenew, the Georgia Tech instructor, who had drownproofed several of the people present.

Conversation rose and fell drowsily. Some of the boys wandered off to look at something under the hood of a car. The women filled plates for the children and helped the youngest, John Steven, to balance himself on a folding chair so it wouldn't collapse under him.

Boiled corn and fresh tomatoes circulated up and down the table. I wished fleetingly that I had opted for homemade peach ice cream and pound cake, lovely summer standbys, and then remembered the heat and was glad there had been no cake baking in my kitchen.

❦ ❦ ❦

We spoke of absent ones. The job hunts of the young, gardens and weather and the Braves. Since we are generally in accord on politics we laughed at the same political jokes and dwelled a little in silent horror on the sexual exploits of two congressmen. But mostly it was easy and peaceful. Family problems and impending decisions and changes were, for one summer evening, shunted aside, not forgotten, just not talked about.

They went home early, bundling sleepy younguns into backseats, trying to latch seat belts over, under or around mayonnaise jars filled with lightning bugs. They called out to one another. "Tell Susan we love her, tell her to come *home*!" . . . "Tell Mary Hill we're so glad what she had wasn't a serious illness." . . . "Tell Norma she should see how the baby's grown!"

The cars stirred up little puffs of dust in the graveled driveway and presently they were gone. I stood barefoot on a flatstone by the back fence and thought of the richness of heat and green growth and summer food and family and was very grateful for it all.

July 26, 1983

A much-traveled friend of mine professes to hate to leave home. She is hardly ever there, but to hear her tell it, she is a confirmed homebody who has a marked aversion to leaving her own bed and board.

"I want to go *home*," she loudly proclaims after touching base with her children and grandchildren, her sisters and cousins and aunts. And home she goes – but not to stay. The next time you look for her, she's off again to some distant place.

It's my contention that I am blood sister to the late Willie Snow Etheridge, who claimed to be ready to go anywhere, anytime. In fact, as I have reported here before, she quoted her husband Mark as saying he was going to put on her tombstone this legend: "The Lord Called Her and She Could Go."

I, too, can go. But you know, there's a little twinge of homesickness that wells up in me, a small wrench of displacement after every departure. I hate it. I would like to be a world traveler.

But there's some odd, perverse streak in human beings that makes them cling to their own nest, their spot in this world. It doesn't make sense, but I believe it must exist in every person, maybe to a greater extent in women who are, of course, the primary nest builders.

🍎 🍎 🍎

When I have to be in town late, I sometimes stay with my daughter and her family, who live in Candler Park, almost as close to downtown Atlanta as you can get. They are warm and welcoming, bless them. They really want me to come. They leave a light on for me, a note that the coffee pot is ready to plug in, a bed turned down, its sheets smooth and cool and inviting. They hang up my clothes and put my overnight bag nearby, hang fresh towels in the bathroom and put a new murder mystery on the bedside table.

Sometime before daybreak, David, the four-year-old, provides the ultimate in hospitality by getting in bed with me to keep me warm and ward off ghoulies and ghosties and long-leggedy beasties and things that go bump in the night. It couldn't be better, visiting my children.

So when I head into the driveway at Sweet Apple and feel that homecoming gladness well up in me, I feel like an ungrateful wretch. Why am I so pleased to see the little slant-roofed house with the rickety screen door that needs to be replaced, the grass that's a week past cutting, the window boxes that need watering?

❦ ❦ ❦

I honestly don't know why I'm so glad to be home. The refrigerator isn't very interesting, yielding up nothing much except cheese, grapefruit juice and one uninteresting beer. The house smells musty and like old wood ashes. (Does it always? I can't remember.)

Once I'm in my old clothes and have polished off the poor fare from the refrigerator, I walk around and look at home with new eyes. In Nova Scotia they wash windows at least once a week. When were mine washed?

At my daughter's house, the trees are bigger and older than mine. I watched the sun come up through a spectacular old elm at the edge of her yard. And yet the prettiest thing my eyes have beheld in trees is the way the sugar maple that supports my hammock is turning rose and gold and vermillion.

Once they get something to eat—and I appease them by serving up a little something extra—the cats settle down to being comfortable, cozy picture-book animals. Papa, the big orange, arranges himself on the patchwork cushion in the kitchen rocker, making the chair move gently while he dozes. The black twins we call the Inkspots take up their posts in the kitchen window boxes, mayhem for the pink begonias but very becoming to them.

So what's so special about home? Darned if I know, but I had that singular delight in being there.

October 11, 1983

*E*very fall a contingent of friends and relatives arrives from the Gulf Coast to do a spot of leaf-looking in our mountains and those of Tennessee and North Carolina. Sometimes I have accompanied them on these trips north, and sometimes I haven't.

This year I couldn't go, and although I missed their good company, I found I didn't miss leaf-looking a bit.

It has come to me belatedly in life that one absolutely spectacularly gorgeous tree is better than a thousand. One view of sourwood and blackgum and sweetgum and sumac blazing in a fence row or across a pasture is about all I can take in. All these years that I have gone forth to collect views and gasp over miles of breathtaking color were, in a word, a waste.

The maple tree by my own well house is almost more than I can comprehend. The dogwoods that screen my log cabin from the road (sort of) are lacquered scarlet and beauty enough.

The other afternoon as I drove into the back yard I caught — for the first time this year — a glimpse of the tiptop of a poplar tree with the sun on it. It was so unexpected, so brilliant, I trod on the brake and sat a few minutes looking at it. Maybe I should have gone to Gatlinburg and Asheville and all the places my friends toured. But somehow I fear I'm not up to it.

The first Edna St. Vincent Millay poem I ever memorized — even, in fact, noticed — was "God's World," and it always comes back at this season, particularly the line about such beauty as "stretcheth me apart."

If you look, really look at one tree, hickory or poplar or maple, it latches on to your heart and you want to cry and sing and maybe, like Millay, pray that not another leaf will fall nor another bird call. You can't be casual and sightseerish about God's world at this time of year.

When I was a little girl, my mother used to walk with me through the autumn woods, less spectacular in south Alabama but still beautiful, and she would sigh and say the fall made her sad.

"The melancholy days are come, the saddest of the year," she would recite, and I was very respectful, thinking if a poet wrote it, it had to be the literal truth. Now I believe that William Cullen Bryant was talking about wintertime and not the blazing carnival of October and November. He went on to cite the "wailing winds and naked woods and meadows brown and sere."

Well, our winds haven't been wailing lately. The woods are far from naked. In fact, there is still a preponderance of green in oaks and beeches. And although I'm not sure if we have any meadows, the fields and open woods are certainly not brown and sere.

Melancholy days? If I weren't a fool about spring and summer and winter, I'd say these are the best days of all — brimming with color and vitality and promise.

They are the days when the faint fragrance of woodsmoke rises from the chimney, when the kitchen smells of apples and cinnamon buns. (Apples from the Aarons' orchard in Ellijay, cinnamon buns by the recipe in the new Mary Mac Tearoom cookbook.) They are the days when you're glad you washed the blankets because they smell faintly of soap and sunshine when you pile them on the bed at night.

We go into summer, some of us, feeling languid and lazy. But autumn and winter's approach are energizers.

There's firewood to be laid in and suddenly a great urgency about cooking. The appetites which flagged during the hot days have turned ravenous. Where's the soup pot? Who is selling really good knuckle bones? It's time to check out the Municipal Market on Edgewood for really substantial viands. How about oxtail soup? How about crackling bread and turnip greens?

No, I don't want to go look at anybody else's trees. My own and those down my road are almost more than I can appreciate. Melancholy days, indeed.

October 31, 1983

*M*y neighbors are getting a fence, an honest hog-wire fence with strands of barbed wire across the top. I applaud that. There are too few old-fashioned keep-in, keep-out fences left in our end of the county. White painted, Virginia horse farm fences abound. There's even a fashion for the old zigzag split rail fence, I regret to say. I have one, given to me by the late attorney Henry Troutman but before they became stylish symbols of suburbia gone country.

Now good field fences are going. So I am cheered that my neighbors, who live down the woods a-piece, are boring fence holes and stringing wire. They will feel secure that their two big dogs, fierce-looking and fierce-sounding fellows, will not trespass or accost travelers in the big road. They will also hope that it will turn back the nocturnal prowlers who seek out lonely country roads for drinking and courting and spreading their garbage. After all, a winding, tree-shaded driveway looks like a country road at night and can be mistaken for one by eyes glazed by alcohol or lust.

So I cheer them on in their fence-building. But for one thing. They will be depriving me of the happy pot-rack of their guineas roaming over my yard, eating bugs and intimidating small, inexperienced snakes. And, worst of all, they will take away one of the most pleasant visitors we've had since we moved to the country – a big handsome rooster with an inner mechanism like a Seth Thomas clock and the voice of an opera star.

The rooster is the delight of my early morning hours, the *countriest* sounding thing since our neighbor Denver Cox stopped gee-hawing a mule in his cornfield. I love that rooster. I feel sorry for people who don't awaken to a rooster's crowing. It is a lightsome, jubilant sound, older than clocks, probably even sundials and far better listening. Even the old poet Blake thought well of roosters. He wrote:
"Wondrous the gods, more wonderous are the men,
More wonderous, wondrous still, the cock and the hen."
My neighbors' hens come with the rooster, of course. They like the viands which even the wintry grass and weeds spread for them. They particularly fancy the seeds which fall from the bird feeder. I think the rooster discovered this. The diligent hens were reticent about coming that close to the house. The big, flamboyant rooster strolls to the kitchen window like he owns the place, samples

the seeds like a hungry guest hitting the dips at a cocktail party, lifts his head and makes his pronouncement.

John Milton, the old poet, gave him credit which I'm sure roosters from time immemorial took unto themselves, banishing night, creating day. The way Milton put it was:

"While the cock with lively din

Scatters the rear of darkness thin,"

My neighbors' rooster does indeed scatter the darkness for me. His "dames" — as Milton called the hens — also make for a little excitement for my grandsons. The other afternoon I heard one cackling, a sound novel and fascinating to David.

"What hurts that chicken?" he asked.

"Hurts?" I said, and then I told him: That lady chicken wasn't whining around about her ills. She was rejoicing in her accomplishments. I grabbed his hand and we went rushing out to the old corn crib (also a gift from Mr. Henry Troutman) to see if we could find her nest.

It's a source of wonderment to David — first that a visiting chicken would leave gifts of eggs, which usually come from the grocery store, and that she would hide them in the weeds or under a lumber pike, like an Easter bunny.

Oh, I'm going to miss the guineas and the hens, but most of all the rooster. My neighbors plan a back gate between our places to facilitate visiting back and forth. I hope they won't notice if I leave it open sometimes — just so he can stroll over and pass the time of day.

February 20, 1984

*I*t's the toughest time of day to be alone, the sunset hour. I've tried it several ways, staying downtown late, asking friends over, going somewhere. I have even taken a book and gone to bed to read out that last time of light on the earth.

That's probably the best because you don't see the setting sun turning the clabber-colored sky back of the woods to rose and gold and scarlet. You don't hear the last sleepy murmuring of the guineas as they select a roosting place or see the birds making forays for a bedtime snack to the feeders. You have, in effect, turned your back on your normal world and fallen headlong into Dick Francis's suspenseful train trip across Canada, as in "The Edge," or into the lovely landscape of the Wapshot clan in New England. (I am now caught up in John Cheever's great twosome, the "Wapshot Chronicles" and the "Wapshot Scandal," since I found at the library that they have been melded.)

🍏 🍏 🍏

But sooner or later, you make yourself return to the old routine, determined that you will not let it get you down, determined to hold memories at bay if you can't cope with them without tears or maudlin sentimentality.

"Sit in the swing," I order myself. "Put your feet up, drink something cool, talk to the animals."

And Papa, the cat, and Kazan, the dog, remembering that it is what we used to call the Children's Hour, come to be with me. Papa climbs into the swing beside me, trailing his long orange tail through the slats in the seat. Kazan sprawls at my feet, a big clumsy paw patting me on the instep now and then.

The color of the sky up beyond where the Johnsons' old chicken house used to be is spectacular, a deeper, more brilliant crimson than I've seen lately. The sky above seems higher and bluer in the waning light, and against a ring of silvery clouds I notice that the hackberry tree has put out a fringe of palest green leaves. The Lady Banksia rose on the bell post is also leafing out, and, for the first time, I notice that the three bridal wreath bushes, brought to me last year from his aunt's old farm in South Carolina by horticulturist Tom Woodham, are snowy white. In the press of a summer of illness and finally death, I had even forgotten planting them.

❦ ❦ ❦

Three white hyacinths have ignored the weedy mess of dried grass and crumpled stalks in the border around them and sent up fragile, exquisite blooms, so perfect, so fragrant it humbles me to see them. Of course, the forsythia is a fountain of gold against the weathered old cabin walls, and the peach trees apparently didn't get the word that the last freeze would do them in. They are a mass of delicate pink.

There's a squawk or two, desultory, sleepy, from the roof of the old corncrib behind me, and I know that the guineas have conferred and voted to settle there for the night. The woods are very quiet, the heat of the sun has given way to evening cool.

I've made it, I reckoned, preparing to go indoors. Then the words of Peter Marshall come back to me: "Do not despair. If you want to be different you may. . . . Therein lies our hope and the hope of the world. . . ."

I don't have much to offer the world, but, for myself, I don't want to be a soggy, mournful widow.

My neighbor had mentioned that she was cooking a fish supper for her newly arrived son and his wife. She had asked me to join them, but I hadn't thought I would. Suddenly I wanted to. I found myself looking for sneakers that would turn the rocks on the road and a flashlight to guide me home after supper. I called Kazan, and we walked along together through the darkening woods. The moon had come out and was very bright. There was already a sprinkling of stars.

March 20, 1989

Branches
of
The Tree

"*H*ow long after her death do you go on grieving for and missing your mother?" asks a letter which came weeks ago. "I know you lost yours and I thought you might be able to tell me. My mother died one year ago and I don't think the ache and sense of loss have eased up one little bit."

The reason I am slow to answer that letter is not that it was covered up on my desk — the usual reason — but because I have been thinking about it and wondering if there is an answer which isn't sappy sounding. My mother who had no use for sentimentality would really hate the way I miss her and scoff at the answer I feel impelled to offer that correspondent.

And that is: Forever.

The reason I'm sure that's the answer is that I've been asking around. One woman told me her mother has been dead for twenty-five years and she thinks of her daily and misses her terribly.

A man who lost his mother when he was ten years old said he finds himself living in the past, dwelling on the first ten years of his life more than any other period. "It's because of her," he says. "She was with me then and her love for me and her care will never be matched by anything else I have received in a generally good and secure life."

Stories about mothers seem to run in schools like mullet. I was moved by Jim Townsend's piece in the March *Brown's Guide.* It's called "Fatback Mystique" and it tells how Jim and his wife and children discovered on a trip to Callaway Gardens many freshly valued things which he knew as a child and was ashamed of.

Growing up in Lanett, he was embarrassed because his mother used a wood-stove and an icebox, instead of owning an electric range and a Frigidaire. "It was galling, terrible that our bathroom was on the back porch while the rest of the world had indoor plumbing and a bathtub," he wrote.

These deprivations, well-known to a lot of us, were made easier by a mother who was apparently a peerless cook and who kept them warm and snug with quilts which he regarded as a poor substitute for store-bought blankets but now recognizes as highly coveted, fiendishly expensive folk art.

John Leonard, writing in *The New York Times,* has a mother who jets around the world in her public relations job with what he calls "a multinational corporation."

But he has memories very much like Jim Townsend's and mine. His mother reared two small boys by working first as a typist, then as a secretary and correcting executives' spelling.

He remembers her in California in 1947 coming home from a long day at the office and hauling a block of ice up the hill to a single room divided by a sheet so that the boys could sleep in their bunkbeds. "My first job was to empty the pan under the icebox each morning after a night of melt. Remember Spam?" asks Leonard.

Alike and different, these two pieces convince me that my answer to the daughter who misses her mother was the correct one. I don't think anybody would promise her that the missing will ever becomes less acute.

Bits and pieces of the past will probably surface as long as she lives. Little expressions, old skills, seasoned attitudes will rise up and smack you when you least expect it and the loss and the ache will be there.

The other day I heard a man say to his wife in either exasperation or awe: "Well, I'll be John Brown!" and I stopped and stared at him in disbelief.

I haven't heard that old expression since Muv said it last now almost four years ago.

March 12, 1980

A letter from a friend about other things ends with wishes for the recovery of our baby and this note: "But, as you know, the quickest route to grief is to be a mother and a grandmother."

It's true, of course, but so is it the quickest route to joy. Everybody has exhausting, bewildering, heartbreaking days. (Another letter from a father extolled the skill and the compassion to be found at Egleston and made me cry a little that it was in vain. His baby died despite all efforts to save him.) But for a parent and grandparent the weariness, the uncertainties and the grief are all leavened by moments of splendor and delight.

My hours at the hospital are brief compared to my daughter's. But they would be interminable except for the occasional little service I can perform for the baby. Feeding him has been of great comfort to me. To hold him in the crook of my arm, to rock him gently in one of the rocking chairs Egleston provides, and to see the competence with which his little jaws work, the felicity with which the adroit little tongue curves around the nipple, fills me with profound delight.

A little body so cunningly made, so artfully able to do the things a baby must do, awes me and makes me hope. If he can make snuffly little puppy sounds against my neck when I burp him, maybe he can learn to breathe properly.

When he stirs restlessly and coughs a racking, choking cough and is eased and comforted when I lift him to my shoulder I feel eased and comforted too.

The same is true of the other children. David, the runabout baby, has been staying in the country with his cousins and Aunt Susan to mind him—a back-aching, mind-numbing job in some respects. But it has high moments of enchantment. All of us hear the sometimes wearisome English language spoken with fluency all day long but when David says a new word we all beam and exchange looks of astonishment and congratulation.

Almost anybody can say "telephone" or "milk" or "ball" or "dog," but it's as if the words were freshly coined and polished to a glorious sheen when we hear them come out of David's mouth.

My neighbor's little lake has always been a pleasure to me but I had not been near it this year—not until Susy and Ted came so their mother could help with our baby crisis. Late the other afternoon because they were there and because Ted said diffidently, "Are you too tired for a swim, 'Tine?" we spent the last sunlit hour on the creek bank. I was too tired for a swim and I sat on a beach towel with my feet in the water and watched them. Ted swam strongly, faster and longer than last year, and I marveled at the growth, the broader shoulders, the longer legs, the capable arms. Susy in her little yellow suit with her red hair in dripping pony tails, capered and splashed and yelled, "Watch me! Watch this!"

❦ ❦ ❦

And it seemed to me that the tranquil lake, a little muddy from the rains, its bank overgrown because its owner is away, never looked lovelier. Nothing ornaments a little pond the way a teen-age boy swimmer and a perky little girl striver do. Birds dipped down for a bedtime bath. July flies turned up in the woods on the hill, horseflies made their noisy landings and takeoffs on the wet backs of the swimmers and I swatted them contently and felt immeasurably enriched because of the moment and the children.

Children and grandchildren are a route to grief, Mary Frances, but ah, the other roads they open for us!

June 30, 1980

*B*y now I guess women have proved that they can do anything. Editors, engineers, inventors, soldiers, sailors, surgeons, prime ministers, miners, scientists — it's all being done by women and it's all easy. I know why. For centuries women have trained on the most challenging task in the world — putting babies to bed.

Putting a baby to bed is one of those things like childbirth or climbing Mount Everest. When the agony is over you forget what it was like. I am three children and six grandchildren down the road, and you could have knocked me over with a feather when I encountered beddy-bye time for David.

His little brother had to go back to the hospital. His aunt had gone home to New Jersey, his other grandparents to Virginia. So David comes to Sweet Apple — to the delight of both of us.

Then bedtime.

🍎 🍎 🍎

Now I know how to handle the ritual things — the late-afternoon capers over the grass in pursuit of a ball or the dogs, suppertime and bath time and hammock time. I know that even for an eighteen-month-old who drinks out of a cup, the bedtime bottle is both a comfort and a soporific. So bottle and baby in hand, I bear him up to bed, bathed and powdered and drowsy (I hope) at eight o'clock.

At first all is quiet and, glowing with self-congratulations, I clean up the kitchen and plan a leisurely bath.

Then I hear the bottle hit the floor, followed by the soft plunk of the teddy bear. The slats of the crib creak complainingly. The air is rent by howls. The house is either on fire or he is being attacked by bears and alligators.

"Let him cry it out," my daughter had instructed me. So I hover at the foot of the stairs, wringing my hands and listening. The tone changes. He is no longer frightened of demons. He is angry. He hollers and screeches and there is accusation in every note. I have done something wrong. I plod upstairs to see. Yep, his diaper needs changing and it is all my fault. He wriggles with delight over this operation, kicking me playfully in the stomach, whooping with pleasure at the sight of me.

Once more I put baby and bottle and teddy bear in the bed and slink down the stairs to sit on the bottom step and listen.

All goes well for a while. He sings and rocks the bed. Then he lets out an experimental cry. I am unmoved. He cries again, neither in anger nor in censure, but because he is sad and lonely, a neglected waif, an orphan, Oliver Twist crying in the night. I swallow hard and dry my damp hands on my apron. Maybe he's winding down, maybe in a minute he'll go to sleep. He doesn't. The piteous wails tear at my heart. Once more, up the stairs.

He is jubilant at the sight of me. He winds his arms around my neck, nestles his head against my shoulder. "Bocka, bocka," he says softly, and I know "rocker" when I hear it and obediently take him to the old Brumby chair on the porch.

Darkness is beginning to settle on the woods. The birds make sleepy sounds. I fill a fresh bottle and stick on a fresh diaper and haul him up the stairs again. It's an uneasy quiet this time, but it is quiet. Waiting, listening, I find my back aching, my legs numb, my clothes drenched in sweat. It seems hours before I dare to tip-toe up the stairs to check. He is a rose and gold Botticelli angel, the most beautiful thing in the world—a sleeping baby. It's nine o'clock.

July 18, 1980

*A*few years ago at a big wrecking yard in Connecticut I bought a splendid two-dollar New York City traffic sign which says succinctly: WALK. I put it in the kitchen window to spur me outward and onward on those mornings when I am prone to dawdle around the house instead of hiking briskly down the road. It turned out that there were a lot of those mornings the sign began to offend me with its nagging. So I moved it to the basement window where I only have to look at it when I am busy washing or ironing or sewing.

It's a great sign and I'm glad to have it. (A friend of mine also paid two dollars for its opposite, a sign which says: DON'T WALK.) But I wouldn't need any old traffic signs to nag me into motion these lovely summer mornings if I could keep a three-year-old at Sweet Apple.

A three-year-old boy named David is the best reason I know to take what the children in our family have always called "Tine's morning walk." He may have reinstituted a custom which has been flagging recently because of weeds in the flower beds and Japanese beetles on the flowers. How can I sally forth for a morning walk when those little sweetheart roses are being gnawed by beetles? How can I turn my back on weeds?

🍎 🍎 🍎

With David it's easy. He puts his baby hand in mine and says confidently, "We walk up the hill now?" And we do, of course. We walk slowly so David can kick a few stones out of the road and occasionally pick one up and throw it. We make many stops. There is a tendril of the little vine we used to call sleeping beauty but which I think is called sensitive plant, trailing over the bank. It is studded with dainty pink pompons, its fragile leaves making a delicate flower to nowhere.

"Come touch it, David," I say. "It will go to sleep."

He stands beside me, one hand clutching my skirt for safety, yellow head bent close to the wild flower.

I rub a finger across a bract of leaves and they promptly close. I hear David take a deep breath.

"Go on, touch it," I invite.

He lifts a dimpled, slightly dirty little hand but he hesitates. The wonder of a plant which goes to sleep when you touch it stays that hand for a long moment or two.

"Go on," I urge. "It won't hurt it. It will wake up again when the sun goes down."

He touches one leaf and then another and another. They fold and he laughs aloud in wonderment.

❦ ❦ ❦

The old country road is rich in splendid sights. A neighbor's dog hears our passing and rushes out to greet us. A mockingbird sets up shop in the old walnut tree at the edge of the pasture and musically assures us that it is going to be a great day. We find dewberries ripening, a June bug there ahead of us, feasting. We find a good stick for walking, a piece of mica like a looking glass, a rusty hinge for keeping.

There is a sandy ditch, just right for a little boy's path and he relinquishes my hand to walk there. Queen Anne's lace and black-eyed Susans make pleasant embroidery of the dusty roadside.

"I pick my mama some frowers?" David offers. (He once got into trouble for picking "frowers" in a neighbor's yard so he is cautious.)

Sure, I tell him, and I help him. He is interested in the flowers' names — not that one of them was named for a queen because he doesn't know about queens, but that it is called lace. We spread the elegant flower head across his palm and he examined it carefully.

"Wace," he agrees with satisfaction.

For me it is a short walk. A three-year-old is too little for very long walks, too big to carry. So we turn back soon.

"Now we go down the hill!" he announces with pleasure, trudging ahead with his "frowers" held aloft like a banner.

June 23, 1982

*O*ne of the things you really can't do well when you have a hand and arm in a cast is to make a creditable chocolate cake. So I went to the bake sale staged by the women of the old Sardis United Methodist Church and if you ever get a chance at one of their chocolate pound cakes, don't delay, grab it up with all speed. We are agreed in our family that even a doting two-handed mother would be hard pressed to do as well.

Almost all else that I tried to do to get ready for the Thanksgiving visit of my children from New Jersey was manageable. Something hot for when they get in, if it's late and cold and they didn't stop to eat on the road, I planned, putting on a pot of stew. Something for all-hours eating for anybody who misses a meal and gets home hungry. So I put on soup bones to simmer, meaty bones that are so expensive I might as well have bought the gorgeous ten-dollar walnut cake from the Sardis ladies.

The in-house family pitched in to help me get four double and three single beds made up a-fresh and a good fire laid in the fireplace. Then everybody else went to bed and left me and my cast up to await. There were many things I could have done, including going to bed and getting in a quick nap before the influx of children and grandchildren. I even put on my nightgown and housecoat with that in mind.

But then I sat down by the fireplace to wait for them and to think about them. The cat Papa came and stretched out in a becoming catty pose on the newly washed slipcover of the best chair. (Why do cats go unerringly to the only down cushion in the house?) I struck a match to paper and kindling and watched the little blue flame leap and catch. The table lamps seemed artificially bright so I lit a candle or two and then a few more. Candlelight becomes white-washed log walls, I thought, settling back to wait. Behind me the old Seth Thomas clock stitched out the minutes, the fire snapped and stirred and the still grave flames of the candles made delicate shadows on the old wood.

You hear a lot about over the hill and through the woods to grandmother's house for holiday visiting but you hardly ever hear how it is at grandmother's end of the line — the excitement, the anticipation, the waiting. They don't sing that grandma, who hates big bright lights in the yard, wishes she had one to guide her children in on a rainy misty night. You don't hear about her uncertainty about her preparations. Edward likes a firm mattress, John would rather be dead than to sleep in a room where there's no television set. Is Susy a soup eater or is she the one who can only abide it if it comes out of a can? The little presents you brought them back from Europe . . . paltry and probably all wrong. Boys practically never need new wallets. What they need is something to go in the old one.

But they are coming! Nothing can detract from that! You stir up the fire and wander to the kitchen. There's a light in the drive. Bird, a local grandson, and a pretty girl come in, laughing and pink-cheeked from the night's dampness. They have come to wait with me, they said. We pull out picture albums, the refuge of the waiting. That's John when he was three, Ted in the funny hat, Susy at her birthday party.

The fire has to be replenished. I make a fresh pot of coffee. Bird takes a turn in the back yard, listening for the sound of their car on the road. It's one of the best things life has to offer you, I think to myself, having family coming home. No rendezvous with a love surpasses it. No urgent or important business engagement. Having your children come home is special and reason for great thanksgiving.

Presently we do hear them in the drive and we go out with flashlights to meet them. There's a hullabaloo of hugging and hauling in suitcases and assigning beds. Suddenly I am very tired. I must go to bed, I say, kissing them all again. I must get my rest for you see, I have this broken arm.

November 23, 1982

"*Y*ou are so lucky to have the teenagers in your family close to you," a wistful letter from a grandmother begins. "My daughter and her family live in Kansas — can you believe it? — and I only see my blessed grandchildren at Christmas and some other holidays."

Don't knock it, I wanted to tell her. An abundance of close-by grandchildren can be heartsease to the lonely, laughs, help and protection. They inspire you to cook, to drag out your favorite books, to rehash your best stories, even to knit them shapeless and ill-fitting sweaters. They can also rob you of sleep, give you middle-of-the-night anxiety and depression, activate your heretofore quiescent ulcer.

That's not just true of the big ones, although when a child gets his driver's license, you have given to fortune your biggest hostage. It's also true of the little ones. Sex rears its dubious head in nursery school and the whole family worries over how much knowledge is wholesome, normal to the growing child, to be expected, and how much is scary and lamentable.

❦ ❦ ❦

Sometimes the distance between Atlanta and Kansas seems enviable to me. At least, that grandmother doesn't face the fevers and tempests of the young until time and distance have cooled them a little.

One of my grandsons went out on a bleak and rainy afternoon to pick up his little brothers at school. Fortunately, he lashed the babies into the back seat with seat belts, because a few blocks from home he collided with another homeward-bound motorist. Nobody was hurt. We all sighed gratefully when we heard that. But he got a ticket and, worst of all, he had to go through that rite so repugnant to the law-abiding citizen. He was, he told me in some pain and outrage, "frisked" and compelled to leave the babies and get in the police car. The officer had not forced these indignities on the other driver.

"Why not?" I asked.

He grinned sheepishly. "I left my driver's license in the pants I took off and I didn't know the insurance card was in the glove compartment."

Not being a mind reader, the policeman did what he had to do. But we all ached a little over it. We all will worry until insurance matters and court hearings are over. Kansas looks good from where I sit.

❦ ❦ ❦

My other grandson had a job to get to and a car that was acting capriciously. He borrowed other cars in the family for two weeks, but the day came when he was going to have to fare forth in his own ailing vehicle. I got up at 4 A.M. to worry over that. I finally solved my problem, if not his, by insisting on following him to town.

Have you ever lumbered along in a truck, trying to keep in view a kid in a sports car? I lost him in traffic about five miles from home and didn't see him again until we reached Brookwood Station. My only consolation was that I hadn't found him stranded by the roadside.

At what they call the Brookwood Interchange, he passed, head high, eyes carefully fixed on the road before him. Who wants to think about or even admit that his grandmother follows him? Better she should be in Kansas.

But there are cheering and reassuring moments. The youngest of them all, John Steven, now almost three, has learned to make songs and plays out of his vicissitudes. When his mother spanked him recently, saying, "I won't have it. . . . I won't have it!" as she walloped him, he borrowed the words for what might be a drama. Ostensibly to himself but loud enough for her to hear, he later sang, "'I won't have it!' the mean girl said."

March 2, 1983

*H*is twenty-first birthday is coming up, and for days I have gone around thinking of that mighty milestone and wishing I could give him something worthy of it. He is the first person to attain twenty-one years in our family for quite a long time and, of course, the first of the grandchildren to reach his majority. It seems important to me, and I know it is important to him, but no gift I can think of seems more than paltry. After all, he already has a Jeep and tools with which to keep it roaring along, and when he wearies of that, he has his fishing tackle. I can't think of anything else he would want.

The truth is that I would like to give him something for his trip through life, something that would make it happier, if not easier, useful if not joyful. Like Christian in *Pilgrim's Progress*, I would like to equip him with the baggage that he can use, not the burden that must roll off his back in the end, but a burden that he bears gladly and finds steadying and strengthening.

❦ ❦ ❦

Love, the most important gift life has, is sometimes a heavy load to bear. It carries with it responsibility and sometimes almost unendurable pain and loneliness. But what life is worth living without love? I hope he will find someone to love more than himself, more than life. At his age he doesn't think much of babies, but I hope the years will teach him that a family, his own family, is what provides the most satisfying of human relationships — that a little baby of one's own is truly wonderous. Parents, brothers, sisters, cousins are worth all the trouble they are to him, an unending source of love and loyalty.

Work that he truly cares about and finds fulfilling would be the second gift I would give him. At his age he is interested in many things, attracted by business and all the wonders of the electronic age, charmed by the feat of money-making. And it might be that he will find work in one of those areas worth pouring his strength and energy and hopes into. Whatever he settles on, I hope it will be work that engrosses him, that seems to him to be a high calling, service somehow to his fellow man.

Equipped with love and good work, his life should be on a good course. But what about faith? Something to believe in, something to trust, something to inspire him to be better than he is, probably should be the foremost gift of all. And yet, faith is hard-won. When you are young you have so many questions, so few answers.

The beliefs of your elders are not always your beliefs. But there may come a time when he feels the exaltation of faith, the comfort of believing.

Beyond these gifts, I would wish him to have patience with his fellow man, humor and the ability to see and feel and taste the small triumphs and absurdities of life. I want him to read. Unfortunately, a child of the television age hasn't the time or the patience for the long hours of poring over old books, dipping into new ones. I am glad that he likes the out-of-doors, that he is at home in the woods and endlessly interested in the natural world. His parents' pleasure in music hasn't infected him yet, but it would be lovely to know that it is there for him and that he will come to it one day.

He began life with wealth he probably never fully appreciated. He had a strong body and a good mind, and all of us love him very much. In a world that is so precarious for so many of the young, he was and is lucky. I don't think he is aware of that, at least not all of the time. Life in a family can be frustrating and irritating. Life at school doesn't always make you feel confident and achieving.

Getting to be twenty-one years old may teach him so much that all the gifts his grandmother wants for him will seem worth attaining to him.

February 6, 1984

*M*y mother always contended that a few chickens and a busy clothesline dressed up a back yard, particularly a country back yard. She felt, I suppose, that they were signs of lively living. I like them, too, but best of all perhaps are little boys to ornament a yard.

My grandsons came to the country. I had house things to do, clothes to change, groceries to put up, supper to start. But their business was with the yard. While daylight lasted they had many tasks to perform, many small excursions to make. I watched them from the kitchen window, their shoes muddy, their fair heads bright in the last of the sunshine, their hands busy.

There were cats to chase, trees to climb, hammocks to swing in. Their old sandbox, a great tractor tire painted green, gift of our former neighbor Glenn Wilkie, was displaced by last summer's upheaval with the septic tank, the sand scattered, its rubber sides twisted. We thought to haul it to the dump but since it has served all our babies so well I have leaned it against a tree and thought about it. They investigated it, examining, one by one, the bleached shells they used to scoop sand, the plastic sifter, the rusting and wheel-less toy truck which their big brother Bird and their Cousin John once played with.

❦ ❦ ❦

When I went out to take them warmer shirts they looked up absently from the heap of things the old tire once accommodated.

"Why is our sandbox tored up?" David asked.

I explained about the septic tank and added, "Since you all are getting so big we thought we might get rid of this old tire. It looks pretty bad."

They looked at me aghast and shouted together, *"No!"* I started to say that it was ugly but I knew better. To little boys, three and five, an old tire is a lovesome thing anyhow. And a monster tire painted green and filled with sand is more beautiful than blooming flowers and splashing fountains. I went back in the house.

From the kitchen window I saw that they had exhausted the possibilities of a sandless sand box and had gone on to other things. John Steven picked a crocus by the back steps and studied it carefully like a botanist looking at some rare unidentified plant specimen. Then he wadded it up and threw it at the cat. David sent the old red wagon caroming down the hill and then ran and pulled it back up the hill. One of the cats came close and got the next ride down the hill.

John Steven came in the house for the announced purpose of drawing me a picture. He sat at the kitchen table with pencil and paper with "creatures" on his mind but then his attention was drawn to the biscuits I was making. He wanted to help me.

I made him wash his hands and then I dusted them with flour and handed him a piece of dough, marveling later that a small, biscuit-sized piece of dough can be stretched to cover so much territory, hands, face, bluejeans, shirt, kitchen floor. With the biscuits — his and mine — in the oven, he wandered off and I watched David through the window

He had found a piece of frayed rope and a big stick and he squatted for long moments, attaching one to the other. That done, he marched purposefully along the slope, towing the stick behind him. Occasionally he looked over his shoulders in much the manner of an Illinois tourist, Florida-bound, checking his house trailer. I couldn't decide what the game was but it satisfied him. He sang a little and stopped and stared at something down in the woods. The stick became a fishing pole, the rain barrel a lake or maybe an ocean.

The sun was low. Rain clouds gathered in the south. John Steven found an old weather-shriveled football under a camellia bush and David abandoned his rope and stick to join his little brother in a spirited throw-and-chase game with the bounceless ball.

From the window I watched their sturdy little bodies fall and tumble on the grass and I hated to call them in to supper. It seemed to me that they adorned the winter-shabby old back yard better than a rose garden or a piece of Venetian sculpture ever could.

February 29, 1984

*T*he day of Jack's death, I thought of the Edna St. Vincent Millay lines, and they stayed with me all week. It's the poem beginning, "Death devours all lovely things." At first it seemed to be true, and then I knew it wasn't, not completely.

Death devours much that is lovely. Gone is the thing about talk, the person waiting at the other end of the road to whom you are eager to talk and who will listen, really listen, to the day's events, the thoughts, the feelings. There was the need to say, "Your college roommate drove over for the funeral . . . These people called . . . There were notes from . . . The sun on the old live oak trees in New Orleans was warm and bright, but there was a breeze . . . Your Aunt Secessia said . . . Your Aunt Lil is 90 and still worrying about a fall garden . . . You'd have loved the airplane they gave us for the trip . . . The grandchildren did just fine as pallbearers . . ."

That "lovely thing" is no more. But human warmth and kindness, and amazing goodness and thoughtfulness, somehow prevail. I didn't know really how much it means to look across a crowded room and see an old friend, a co-worker from years ago, to feel hands reaching out, arms enveloping, tears on other faces.

❧ ❧ ❧

I didn't suppose that doctors, conditioned as they are to death, would cry. I wasn't prepared for the almost family closeness of people at the hospital, who offered a quiet room, telephones, a shoulder to lean on, time for shocked and stricken relatives to reel from the impact of death and somehow collect themselves.

As an only child with few relatives until I had children of my own, I wasn't geared to the wonderful strengthening thing of families rallying. They came from Texas and Louisiana and Mississippi, not knowing death was imminent but knowing he was in peril. My own children came from New Jersey and Florida, driving long hours to get here and set out food and take a turn at the hospital and chauffeur his mother and his aunt around.

And then, when it was over and we were back from the funeral, they saw the task I had forgotten. His office had to be cleared out and emptied. His clothes and all the oddments of living that a person collects . . . did I want them packed up, given away, moved so that I wouldn't see them and remember all the days that are left to me? No, I said, and then I saw his old shoes by the back door, and I knew that I couldn't take much more. An old shoe is so personal, so much like the man who wore it, so poignant in shape and color and size.

Go ahead, I told them. Take his things away.

❦ ❦ ❦

It was a tough task for them. They had memories, too. But they went through files and closets and dresser drawers, often laughing and joking among themselves at something he had said or done, sometimes deferring to me about saving some scrap of paper, a letter, a picture.

It's by no means true, as Millay wrote, that death devours all lovely things. It breaks hearts and devours a staggering amount of what is dear and gives meaning to life. But it is not altogether ruthless, either.

As the poem tell us, "presently every bed is narrow." Eventually, of course, I came to remembering that other poem of Millay's, which has come to mind many times through the years. It is called "Lament," and in it a mother tells her children their father is dead. It ends:

Life must go on
And the dead be forgotten.
Life must go on though good men die.
Anne eat your breakfast,
Dan take your medicine.
Life must go on.
I forget just why.

So life goes on for the two families that claimed Jack Strong as their own.

November 30, 1988

A person I cared for used to say I was "a tough old turkey." He meant it as a compliment, and I was glad to have it — or any compliment. Although an old turkey isn't exactly a luminous bit of imagery, it's not bad to be tough. In fact, it's better than being a sappy, self-pitying, quivering mess of jelly.

Life exacts toughness from us rather often, it seems. We are instructed from childhood to be independent, to paddle our own canoes, to stand up to adversity. And sometimes the only way we can do this is by turning mean and shrewish, as I have more times than I like to count recently.

But there comes inevitably, at the Christmas season, moments when whatever toughness you have built up dissolves totally. An unexpected shaft of tenderness or beauty strikes your heart, and you find yourself bawling like a fool.

The other day I went into our neighboring Woolworth's to shop for things to be put into a stocking to be sent overseas by the USO. (I hope you did that, too.) I saw an old woman in the cold weather gear the old women I have known always get together — head scarf, old coat, galoshes with cotton stockings showing above them. She stood at a counter of Christmas decorations and her old hands, spotted and veined and knotted with arthritis, fingered a sheaf of gold tinsel. She seemed lost in a dream as she separated the strands of gold one by one and ran them through her fingers.

🍒 🍒 🍒

For a few moments, I stood in the aisle while more single-minded shoppers pushed and jostled by me. The sight of her seemed to catch in my throat, and I was afraid I would cry. I don't know if she bought the glittering geegaw, but I know her hands loved it and maybe her heart remembered a happier day.

A little later, my grandson, who came to spend the night, picked up his guitar as we sat by the fire. I was reading and didn't pay much attention as he trifled around with some old folk tunes. Occasionally, he would lift his sweet young voice in song, cocking an eyebrow at me to see if I wanted to join him.

"You know 'Old Rugged Cross'?" he asked at last.

I thought I did, but I foundered on the verses and went to the organ to look for a hymm book. He leafed through it, and we sang along together on several old favorites before he returned to "Wildwood Flower" and "Git on Board, Little Chillun" and a wonderful one about a fellow who worked in a coal mine and wanted to be buried there where "the sun never shines and the rain never falls."

When his fingers began to tire, he poked up the fire and started to put up his guitar.

"Do a Christmas one," I suggested.

He strummed aimlessly for a few seconds, and then the melody of that loveliest of Christmas carols emerged.

"Silent night, holy night, all is calm, all is bright . . ."

He sang, and it was like he was a little boy again riding home from school with me. I dared not try to blend my raspy, tuneless voice with his. When he struck the final chords with a gentle flourish and looked up, his young man's face was taut with distress.

"I didn't mean to make you cry," he said contritely.

"No, oh, no!" I cried, wiping my eyes and blowing my nose. "You don't make me cry. I just . . . I don't know . . . some things just get to you, don't they?"

You can become conditioned to kindness, just as you can become conditioned to pain, I suppose. The outpouring of sympathy and comfort people have offered my family in recent weeks eventually came to be something I could handle with calm gratitude. I will never get thanks said to everybody, but I have decided it's all right to wait a while with your friends.

And then I walked back in the back yard at dusk and saw the most beautiful burfordi holly shrub I have ever seen, pruned so that every branch holds a rich cluster of deep red berries. It came from good friends who were on call, they wrote, to come and dig the hole when I was ready to plant it.

Even tough old turkeys cry sometimes.

December 18, 1988

From Seed
&
Soil

*M*y neighbor stopped at our country mailboxes and pulled out a bright windfall of seed catalogs for all of us. "I'm not *ready* for this yet!" she wailed. She spoke for a lot of us. Despite our garden editor Roy Wyatt's get-ready advice, it's too soon, too soon. We need some more winter, some renewal and recovery time. I went to church and heard the choir sing a song I'd never noticed before, all about the beauty of the earth under a blanket of snow. A-ha, I thought, Fletcher Wolfe, the music director, also makes a bid for more winter.

But it was warm in my back yard with a tentative, indecisive little rain falling. A perfect time, I knew, for a small cleanup fire, the one I didn't get around to last fall. Most dried stalks and grass and all fallen leaves are welcome on the compost pile, but the obnoxious weeds and the stalks of vegetables most likely to harbor pests and diseases go into a little blaze at the edge of the garden.

My heart wasn't in it. A rainy afternoon is intended, I hold, for trying a new recipe or a bit of fireside sitting and reading and knitting. But the arrival of seed catalogs is a summary call to action. It takes a stronger-minded person than I am to dawdle by the fireplace when Burpee and Parks and Wayside and Savage and all that crowd sound a clarion call that the hour is at hand to order, to prepare, to clear the slate for spring.

So I put on a sweater, which I shortly had to shuck, and went out to join the issue with dead grass and soggy leaves. Everywhere there were reminders of things I hadn't done — the larkspur and poppies and cornflower seeds I didn't get in the ground in late summer, the bulbs I didn't plant. But it was good work. It's one of the best things about our climate, I suppose, that dead-of-winter day when you can work outside in comfort.

My little fire sent up a tendril of fragrant blue smoke. Our cat Papa went ahead of me into a thicket of weeds and tawny, amber-colored grass to check it out for wild beasts. Finding none, he took shelter from the desultory rain under the car and watched me with yellow-eyed disapproval. (Papa holds to the conventional wisdom that a cat's place is by the fireside on a January afternoon.) But the longer and harder I worked the more I enjoyed it.

In January you can see and feel the shape of the earth better than at any other time. The poison ivy is quiescent. The ground ivy, if not dormant, is at least temporarily at bay. The crisp brown leaves and stems of last summer's flowers relinquish their hold on the earth easily. You see things you hadn't noticed before or ignored because you were busy.

Of the ten hemlocks I ordered from the Market Bulletin and planted at the edge of the woods, one survives and is in exuberant health. The baby holly tree which we carelessly stuck out too close to a clump of pines and a greedy wisteria vine, is holding its own. The rosa rugosa from a Long Island beach needs to be divided and moved before it crowds out the peonies and marches on the bean patch.

And the little chinaberry tree which volunteered in a flower bed has taken a running start and is five feet tall. Descendant of a long line of chinaberry trees which have grown around Sweet Apple cabin, it lives when others have died. I want it. An old country house devoid of chinaberry trees, even if you have a hammock instead of a washpot and tubs to go under them, seems all wrong.

The answer was to move it. A friend manned the shovel, seeking out roots which went to China. We hauled the cool, freckled trunk to a clearing in the woods near the road and hacked out a hole in the root-laced earth. The soil is dark and sweet-smelling there and as I helped to steady the tree and pat it in place, I knew at last what I've been trying to postpone. It's time — and I am ready — to read the seed catalogs.

*M*y friend who grows spectacular marguerite daisies was surprised to hear that I was slogging around in potting soil trying to start marguerite seeds. Why don't I just wait and buy the plants? Well, I haven't seen any marguerite plants south of East Hampton, Long Island, and when I got out of the car to try to buy some there the nursery was closed.

So I ordered off and I've got quite a lot of marguerite seeds, a dozen or so buried in wet potting soil in little pots in the basement, swathed in plastic, lovingly and prayerfully checked every day of the world. The others I will sow somewhere in the yard when spring comes, if ever.

But to get back to sowing your own seeds. I believe in it. I also believe in acquiring plants any other way you can — buying, begging, swapping. My plants are never as handsome as those started by my neighbors, Gwen and Roy Wyatt. In fact, a lot of times my plants don't even show. I plant the seeds and they take a powder on me.

But, ah, when you do plant a seed and get a plant, the satisfaction, the pleasure, the excitement of gardening is all there.

The packaged potting soil I have been using is troublesome. It has so much peat in it it's hard to get it wet. I'm thinking about going back to the system of mixing my own but that was troublesome, too. I baked sand in the oven to kill whatever bugs cause damp-off, I measured and stirred with the zeal of some mad alchemist. The results weren't sure-fire. But I did get a lot of plants — so many one year I had trouble finding yard space for them.

Would that it would happen again! Would that the white nicotiana would spring up with great alacrity and be eager to get its feet out the door about late April.

And how about those Irish lace marigolds? I have never planted them before but they looked so pretty in the catalogs I ordered some and spent a gloomy cold Sunday afternoon sifting one seed at the time into holes made in the potting soil with a pencil. The old-fashioned marigolds which some of you have been thoughtful and generous about sending are easy. I know they'll grow and bloom and be an ornament to my summer days, no matter what mistakes I make with them. The late Sen. Everett Dirksen had a good idea when he campaigned to make the marigold the national flower. There's no easier or happier bouquet of beauty in this world.

On the other hand, has anybody tried sweet woodruff? Or do you dare to plant your basil seeds in February and March in flats in the basement instead of in May in the garden? I went the basement route and now I go down the stairs every morning, turn on the light and lift the plastic, calling out like some Jane Austen heroine on a windy moor, "Basil? Sweet Basil! Where are you?"

Old Basil hasn't made an appearance yet but there are tiny green shoots showing among the bachelor button seeds. And I think something is stirring beneath the black soil where I planted those Roma tomatoes. (Got the idea of Romas from my neighbor Libby Stambaugh, who sticks them in her flower beds and makes wondrous sauces out of them.)

One of my favorite garden writers, Josephine Neuse, gave up on petunia seeds as "too fussy" and waited and bought her plants. I subscribe to that plan except in the case of the old-fashioned petunias, which come back year after year. I ordered some of those seeds from the Market Bulletin and scattered them over the surface of a foil pie pan full of dirt. If they don't show I think it means I won't have perennial petunias. The word for gardeners, I guess, is to try, keep trying—and hope.

March 2, 1982

*M*y old friend Ollie Reeves may have been the first person to tell me that we all have greater riches than we deserve.

I was a blessing-counter from way back, of course, having been reared by a woman who eternally reminded you that if you weren't grateful for what you had (knock on wood!), things could worsen up fast.

But until Ollie once said of himself that he enjoyed success and pleasures that far over-reached his talents and his efforts, I had never really thought about it. I suppose I figured any good thing that came my way was my due.

This spring I have thought a lot about the unearned, undeserved, unmerited wonders of nature. Sure, you plant and you make a stab or two at maintenance. You might even work pretty hard at your patch of earth to no apparent avail. And then there will come a spring like this one when every single thing outdoes itself in beauty.

We were away at the beach for a week, and I came home to a tangle of weeds and unkempt grass. Have you ever known a lawnmower that wouldn't conk out the day you have a big strong boy there to run it?

I had a terrible sense of pressure building in me since I saw how benign the weather was going to be. I, who had been telling everybody that it was too early to plant in April, that it was bound to freeze on Easter, that late May or June offered the optimum planting dates.

Suddenly, somewhere in Barbour County, Alabama, it struck me that we're well into summertime and I haven't even got beans in the ground. Those flower seeds, where on earth did I hide them this year?

The car was barely in the yard before I was on the ground, racing around, trying to figure if there was enough light left to begin my wholesale farming immediately. There wasn't. It was 8 p.m. by the new time — just enough light left for me to see what was there, blooming with a heart-stopping beauty that nearly brought tears to my eyes.

The Cherokee rose on the well-house, white, golden-hearted blossoms against old gray shingles, was the most beautiful thing I ever saw. I stood for moments, looking at it, choked up with a rush of gratitude for such bounty, such undeserved riches.

The weigelia was the same — long fronds of pale pink flowers, underplanted (not by me but by accident) with purple spiked ajuga, all in full bloom. Some things had bloomed and faded. The yellow Lady Banksia rose on the other side of the well-house was well past its best. But on the back fence, where I planted it years ago and it languished, the Peace rose was loaded with buds!

How did they get there? Why did they choose this year to offer up a generous, profligate bouquet of blossoms when they've been squinchy all these years? I have no idea. It must be, as we used to say of all natural phenomena in the country, time for the world to come to an end.

Well, if the world wants and needs to come to an end, it's all right with me if it does so when the peonies are opening and the irises are unfolding flags of color from their green satin sheaths. What better time than when the pink climbing rose by the breezeway door (the one so chary with its blossoms up to now) has decided to bloom and bloom and bloom? The rhododendron is showing color, the larkspur are ten inches tall, the little fig tree is fat and green and full of promise.

The unpaid-for, undeserved accomplishments in my backyard had me so moved I had to help unload the car by flashlight.

And then I remembered the four o'clock seeds I planted weeks ago and went out to see if they were up. They are not. But the precious white ones I put in peat cups (too rare to scatter willy nilly in the ground) had two leaves each. Such a spring I never saw and may never see again!

April 29, 1981

*T*here's something to be said for being a late starter in the garden in the spring. My old-time country neighbors regard it as simple common sense to wait until the ground warms up before getting anything but cool weather crops in the ground. I have known many of them to wait until June 1 to set out their tomatoes and sow their beans and peas. City people are the early birds, they will tell you up at Chadwick's store.

It isn't foresight which made me late this year. It was simply that the weather and I couldn't get synchronized. When it was ready for yard work I wasn't and vice versa. Visitors and out-of-town trips and various distractions large and small conspired to divert my attention while the weeds grew and the seeds I ordered bided their time in the freezer compartment of the refrigerator.

There is no way, I have wailed to my kith and kin, that I can now catch up on all the chores that are suddenly overwhelming me on that small patch of earth. I am sunk, the yard is going to be an arid wasteland this year, we won't have a homegrown tomato or a bean to our names. Oh, wurra, wurra!

But with gardening, as with practically everything on earth, the secret is, of course, to begin. You very likely won't get everything done but if you make a start you'll get *something* accomplished and that's better than beating your breast and howling in self-pity and frustration.

So I started. One sunny morning I vowed to let the breakfast-hungry fend for themselves, to let beds and dishes go and to get at those weedy tangles in the front yard, where I meant to have the beginnings of a cottage-type perennial garden. The first deterrent, believe it or not, was a white guinea hen on a nest. My neighbor's raucous, loud-mouthed guinea for once didn't screech and berate me like a rusty-lunged old harridan when I approached. She sat quietly on a nest in the midst of day lilies, Sweet William and coreopsis and eyed me with mute appeal. (I found out later she had 20 eggs beneath her white feathers!)

Well, that took care of that portion of the patch. I can't imagine anybody so bent on weeding she would dispossess a guinea and her offspring, can you?

So I turned my attention to the two beds nearer the house. At first they looked pretty hopeless. Grass and weeds had swallowed them up in a tide of tough green.

But the sun was warm and golden, a bobwhite called from the woods, my cat Papa stretched out on the stone step for company and I knelt and dug. Creeping Jenny was the worst. Chickweed second and ajuga, which I meant to be between the stepping stones, spread a near-impenetrable carpet over everything. But patience and an occasional epithet saw me through and I began to see that great boon to any garden — the forgotten, unexpected treasure. I had complained to my friend Betty Drummond, who gave me petunias which reseed themselves, that they weren't doing that this year. No sign of them, I told Betty sadly. I was wrong. They had merely moved. Instead of being at the edge of the bed, where I planted them, they had come up in the shade of hollyhocks and spiderwort. There were a dozen of them, tender little plants of a deep and lusty green. I moved along with my hand rake and weeder. The next thing I discovered was a whole colony of marguerite daisies, the very ones which didn't do a thing for me last year. They were so smart and obliging to have survived and to surprise me thus, I thought.

The work went well for a while — and then came the rain. But that's all right. It's good when I get to it and just think, if I had weeded earlier, I might have wasted a lot of things I treasure.

May 18, 1983

*T*here are no more provocative or intoxicating words spoken to any gardener than these: "The roses are blooming."

As I have mentioned here once or twice, roses are not my strong suit. In fact, they have fought me hip and thigh for many years. I have starved my children to buy rose bushes with the grocery money. I have fed those ornery bushes cow manure so expensive it might as well have been rubies or the blood of snow white doves. I have read books, interviewed the experts and come to the conclusion that some can grow 'em, some can't.

So I gave up, sadly, reluctantly, but no less a surrender. Roses hated me.

Now what do you know, roses have bloomed in my yard this year! Maybe not spectacularly, maybe nothing to set pulses hammering at the Atlanta Botanical Garden. But they have bloomed. The old Peace, which I planted twenty years or more ago and yearned to see in its glory, has cut loose and filled the back fence with blooms.

The Pink Spice has acted like a florist flower, many long-stemmed buds so firm and velvety they should cost twenty-five dollars each.

The little Golden Showers climber, which is likely to be malnourished among the tree roots and the bushes around the well-house, climbed up and extended to me half a dozen butter-yellow, deeply fragrant blooms. The climbing Cecile Bruner scattered diminutive pink flowers on the other side of the well-house roof.

Such riches I never dreamed of. And then the New Dawns! Has everybody else already discovered the charms of this small pink-blossomed climber? I think I saw it on a trellis in Ryan Gainey's yard, and, like all highly successful gardeners, he was deprecating its cultivation. Nothing to it, he must have said. Stick it in the ground and forget it.

Only such talk as that would have impelled me to stop by the Thomasville Nursery on my way to Florida some months ago and invest in New Dawns. I planted them without hope — and forgot them. Imagine my surprise to find two of them draping bouquets of rosy buds and blossoms along the old rail fence.

While I was deciding I am probably a horticultural genius and the roses have taken off because they know they have met their match, my eye fell on a bit of pink in the tall grass and weeds at the other end of the fence. My goodness, I had forgotten that I bought and set out three roses on that fence and one on the chimney back of the house! Neglected, forgotten, weed-choked, they had risen above it all and started blooming.

There may be more rewarding occupations for a woman at the crack of dawn these mornings, but I opt for liberating roses.

It has been chilly in the early hours of the day, so I wrap up in whatever's handy and go forth with hoe and clippers and knee in obeisance before the shiny leaves, the fragile flowers of roses that seem bent on survival. The earth is damp, the fragrance of the honeysuckle almost overpowering and two brown thrashers take up their posts in the old persimmon tree to see if I'm going to unearth anything appetizing. I wish they ate honeysuckle — or that something did — but it is so beautiful, so sweet-smelling I am almost reconciled to letting it share the roses.

If we had to buy honeysuckle, we would certainly fertilize and water it as if it were some exotic beauty. It's just one of nature's gifts that come free.

As a result, honeysuckle is often damned as a pest, grubbed out of the earth and hauled away as if it were kudzu. And what do some of us do with roses? Kneel before them and risk snakebite and brier scratches and poison ivy before sunup.

May 19, 1989

*Y*ou know the kind of person who always catches any disease they read about? Well, I'm worse. I'm the kind of person whose plants come down with any malady I happen to hear about.

The other day a woman and I were having a pleasant gardening chat, congratulating ourselves on having just come through maybe the most beautiful spring the world has ever seen. We extolled dogwood and iris and rhododendron and peony. We said that never, never had we seen daffodils and tulips and Johnny-jump-ups acquit themselves with such style.

Suddenly she said, "What gets on hollyhocks?"

"Huh?" I said, abruptly jolted out of dirt road Pollyanna-ing.

"Something is eating mine," she went on. "Don't you have that trouble? Every hollyhock I have set out is perforated."

🐛 🐛 🐛

It was news to me. I thought hollyhocks were among the most durable flowers in the world. Their only drawback is that you have to plant them this year for next year's bloom, and I'm always too little and too late. But I did start some seeds in the house along about March and I have set a few of the cunning little plants out in the front yard, having a mental picture of the cottage-like glory of hollyhocks against log wall and rock chimney.

Not knowing what ails hollyhocks, I wasn't much use in the rest of the conversation, until another woman said she heard that dishwater is a great boon to hollyhocks.

Sure, I agreed. That must be just exactly what V. Sackville-West was talking about when she said many of the old-fashioned flowers excelled in cottage gardens because of the housewifely custom of dumping soapy water on them.

"All that grease?" put in another gardener.

"Not the grease," I mused. "Just the soapy water."

"I'm committed to my electric dishwasher," another voice put in, ending the conversation.

So I hurried home and rushed out and looked at my hollyhocks, the little darlings. They were thread lace and drawn work! Hardly a leaf that wasn't holey.

Roy Wyatt, our gardening editor, is my authority on most plant life. What he doesn't know about growing things his wife Gwen does know. So I presented my lacy hollyhocks for his inspection.

"There's a little white fly," he said thoughtfully. "Have you seen it flying around?"

❧ ❧ ❧

If it flies, hops or crawls I have seen it this spring. All that beauty we were talking about didn't come without cost. It has been the buggiest season I can ever remember. When I go out to count bean sprouts every morning, winged traffic swarms over me, filling my eyes, nose and mouth and causing me to jump around in my nightgown like Rita Hayworth doing the shimmy.

It really makes me mad that all I had to do was hear about hollyhock eaters, and, *voila*, I catch an infestation.

So these mornings find me mixing up soapsuds in the mop bucket. Not to mop the bathroom or kitchen, of course. (Who wastes these gold and green mornings with such activity as that?) My soapsuds are headed for the hollyhocks. I only wish I had planted them by a kitchen window so all I would have to do would be to open the window and pitch.

May 24, 1982

*I*t was only a little fig tree. I think it may have cost a couple of dollars at a recent nursery sale. As I lugged it in its gallon can toward the house, thinking where I would plant it, I had the most wonderful feeling about it—a sense of oneness with the earth and all the people who have written about it.

For, of course, the fig tree holds an old and respected place in the literature of the world. How would Eve have clothed herself after that disastrous flight into knowledge and sin if the Garden of Eden hadn't had at least one fig tree?

My little tree, as small as it is, already boasts two figs. And as I set it down and stood back looking at it, I thought it had a right saucy look—a horticultural smart aleck who knew its pedigree and where it belonged in the world. Bearing yet!

❧ ❧ ❧

The ground was as hard as granite, and it took me a while to dig a hole but it was good work. The sun had vanished behind a cloud, and there was promise of rain in the air. The sack of cow manure I had hauled up was not deodorized, as the label promised, but smelled richly of the place of its origin, a barnyard somewhere. I inhaled and dug in and thought of poor Mother Eve standing there in Eden in her fig leaf apron hearing those fateful words: "In sorrow thou shalt bring forth children. . . . In the sweat of thy face shalt thou eat bread, till thou return unto the ground; for out of it wast thou taken; for dust thou art, and unto dust shalt thou return."

There's a theological theory that she got us into our troubles, but maybe we also inherited from her a pleasure in the earth and the necessity of sweating to get our bread. Shoot, I like digging in the earth, and I bet Eve found in it a consolation for some of those troubles that descended on her.

When Cain and Abel started cutting up acting like hippies or terrorists or, as we used to call them in a more innocent day, juvenile delinquents, Eve may have watered the fig tree with her tears and then felt better about everything.

"While the earth remaineth," I thought, "seedtime and harvest, and cold and heat, and summer and winter, and day and night shall not cease."

With the tree in place, watered and fertilized and mulched, I turned over a bucket and sat down on it to admire my handiwork. Its older brother, my three-year-old fig tree, has overreached itself. It had two crops this year—three figs back in the early summer, eight figs now, two of them dark brown and dripping with sweetness. What a harvest!

❦ ❦ ❦

The Bible thought well of the fig tree. It must have been one of the few trees which reliably grew and bore in that hot and arid land. In the book of Micah, there's a suggestion that owning your own land with a fig tree upon it is a great thing: "They shall sit every man under his vine and under his fig tree." And practically the same thing in Maccabees: "Every man sat under his vine and under his fig tree."

One of the first Edna St. Vincent Millay books I ever acquired was called "A Few Figs from Thistles," and I was trying to remember how she justified that. But it is, I suppose, an example from a line by William Butler Yeats: "grapes from thorns and figs from thistles."

Folklore hasn't neglected fig trees either. There is an old theory that fig trees only flourish close to houses where they can hear the sound of human voices — raised in conversation and laughter and maybe squabbling too, for all I know. But I'm not going to let any unpleasant words be spoken around my fig trees. Not that I'm superstitious, but then there's no need to take a chance.

September 20, 1980

*M*y neighbor, Verda, reminded me that it was time to start the narcissus bulbs in pebbles and water for Christmas, maybe even Thanksgiving, blooms.

She had the bulbs, satiny brown nubbins of locked-in beauty and fragrance. I collected the little rocks and some old bowls saved through the years and arrived at her house just before sunset.

We put a layer of the pebbles in the bottoms of the bowls, snugged in the bulbs and anchored them with pebbles almost to the brim of the containers. The sun lay sheets of gold against the western side of the house, the sweet smell of hay rose from what used to be the front pasture, and we stood a moment admiring the deceptive beauty of a villainous poison ivy vine, all scarlet and gold as it climbed a poplar trunk.

"Thank you for remembering narcissus," I told Verda as I was leaving. And I meant it. Of all the little rituals of the season — the getting ready, laying by, putting up for winter — starting the narcissus bulbs is one of my favorites.

The mystery of bulbs never ceases to bemuse me. How can something so plain and unprepossessing contain such blooms, such fragrance? They did their own preparation for winter, laying by white flowers and their fresh, sweet scent for days when the trees will be bare and the winter winds will howl. My mother always started narcissi in the house in the fall and the memory of them is as durable to me as the other scents of home — turpentine and Winesap apples and sweet potatoes baking.

Ralph Austen, in a 17th century book about fruit trees, wrote:

"Sweet perfumes work immediately upon the spirits, for their refreshing, sweet and healthfull ayres are speciall preservatives to health, and therefore much to be surpprized."

It is not my contention that paper whites blooming in a soup tureen will improve my health in November or December, but I don't see why not. Where I grew up, narcissi bloomed in the yard — the earliest flower we had — but it suits me very well that I don't get very early ones at Sweet Apple. I'm not even one of those ecstatic admirers of the crocus. For one thing, they come in such ugly colors — purple and orange, ugh! Let the yard flowers stay in their places in the ground until spring comes. I don't like to see a fool, before-handed crocus sticking out of a snow bank.

But in the house . . . is there anything lovelier or more surprising than a bowl full of lilies of the valley blooming on Christmas Day beside a chair drawn up to the fire?

❦ ❦ ❦

Just as I don't exult in crocus, there are people who loathe the smell of the paper white narcissus. (Margaret Mitchell associated cape jessamine with funerals, remember?) Some people are sickened by all the jasmine fragrances. A woman I know cries when she smells violets because they remind her of her mother's death in a roomful of them.

Many people dislike the astringent smell of marigolds. A bowl full of hyacinths too close can overpower you, I admit.

Even the scent of roses is depressing to some people who associate it with unhappy times. Since I'm a poor rose grower, I don't have to worry about that, and when the Cherokee by the wellhouse elects to bloom — not every year and not profligately, mind you — I think it is the freshest, most evocative smell in the world.

The truth is that three or four months from now we'll all be tired of winter and grateful for anything smelling of the earth and green-growing things. I read of a gardener who told her husband spring mud smelled so wonderful she wanted to run outdoors and roll in it. She lived in a section of the country where mud bespoke spring thaw. We have plenty of it all winter so I don't value it much, but the savor of most growing things affects me as it did Gerard, the famous herbalist: "Rejoyceth the heart."

October 10, 1983

*N*orth Georgia's countryside looks like Brigadoon these early mornings with the mist rising like spun silver over farm ponds and the sassafras blazing crimson and gold in the fence rows. Almost any minute now we can look for the first killing frost of the season and everybody I know is caught up in that old seasonal indecision: Shall I bring in the geraniums tonight or can I wait a while?

Naturally, we all hate to bring in the few things that are left blooming in the yard until the last possible moment. That's the reason the night the first killing frost is predicted catches more people than I supposed loping over the yard frantically looking for shovel and flower pots. I thought I was the only one who put this job off to the eleventh hour but some highly skilled gardeners of my acquaintance also confess to procrastination.

❦ ❦ ❦

What to do with those geraniums, sultanas and begonias when you have dug them up from bed, border, tub and window box? The experts give you so many alternatives you may find yourself like me, wasting winter heat on a bunch of plants which grow leggy and anemic before next spring. That's what happens when I put everything in pots and set them up on the window sills and in the basement. My friend Andrew Sparks has a different system. He snips off cuttings and puts them in glasses of water on his windowsills, where, he promises, they will establish fine sustaining root systems by planting time and all you will have to do is transfer them to the dirt outside.

Dean Mansell of the vast Roswell family who have raised and sold produce for many years, remarked the other day that he loses his geraniums every year. He has an aunt who simply pulled hers up and hung them upside down in a cool dry place. Come the spring, she set them out and jumped back. They were off and running.

"Yeah, I've heard of that system," I said, "but the one time I tried it nothing lived. Maybe the shed got too cold."

But now I'm ready to try again — on the advice of still another expert, this one a bonafide horticulturist, Don Hastings. In his Southern Garden Club monthly newsletter, which is published at Norcross and is a continuing delight to me, Don devoted half a page to saving geraniums this month.

❦ ❦ ❦

Praising the contributions this old-fashioned flower makes to the summer beds and planters and noting the high cost of replacing them, Don urged gardeners to consider saving their plants from year to year.

"In early October," he wrote, "make a number of 4 to 6 inch cuttings from the freshest growth. Root them in pellet peat cubes or trays of vermiculite. After good roots have formed, pot the young plants in 6-inch plastic or clay pots to carry over the winter in a bright sunny window."

And then to the tricky, dry root method: "Dig the older stock plants or remove them from their pots and lay them on their sides on newspaper where they can dry for several days. After the soil around the roots is dry, but not bone or powder dry, shake off all the soil that comes away easily. Now wrap the roots in plastic bags and store in a cool 50-60 degree place during the winter. Store them lying down, and in moderate light.

"In the spring, cut them back and pot them to force fresh, new growth. Put these vigorous plants outside after danger of frost has passed."

Young Mr. Hastings has just returned from spending three weeks in Egypt, where he is teaching the locals how to grow fresh vegetables. His advice on saving old geraniums should be infallible so any minute now I'm going to close my eyes and start yanking up those faithful summer friends and put them away for a long winter's rest.

October 27, 1980

*W*hen my mother was alive, one of the things I always brought back from a visit to her house was an armload of magnolia boughs. If you don't have any furniture, a jugful of these handsome branches dresses up a bare room. If you have been to the Salvation Army and Goodwill stores lately and have too much furniture, there's still a place for those gleaming green leaves—either on the mantel or in front of the sooty and unsightly empty-of-embers fireplace.

So I got in the habit of bringing back many magnolias from her yard, detouring to South Georgia swamps and Florida roadsides when my itinerary changed. Since the magnolia grows wild down there, it doesn't seem an affront to break a branch off first one and then another—an unthinkable act of violence in my own yard where two pampered, so slow-growing magnolias would brook no such looting.

From magnolias, I moved to bay leaves and, of course, at Christmastime, there is always need of cedar in the house. Since I have been visiting my favorite little island off the coast of Florida, I find it necessary to haul home an occasional sprig of wild rosemary and, if I can beat the birds to it, a branch of the red-berried yaupon.

All of this avaricious interest in roadside horticulture enlivens many a long drive through North Florida and South Georgia. I hardly ever stop, but I peer into the swamps and pine woods and spot lots of reasons for stopping, if it ever works out.

My latest reason is a sudden craving to equip my yard with a gallberry brush broom before spring. Now I know "brush broom" sounds redundant, but I can't help it; that's what they were called in South Alabama when I was a child. And every householder with a smidgen of pride had several for keeping hard-swept yards free of leaves and twigs and sometimes chicken droppings. Yard sweeping was a weekly chore, falling, as I recall, on Saturdays, so when after-church company came by, the premises would look neat as a wet-combed head.

There may have been store-bought yard brooms then. I don't remember ever seeing one. There may have been makings superior to the gallberry.

But we had gallberry bushes in super abundance in the woods and at the edges of fields and swamps, and they made splendid brooms.

❦ ❦ ❦

I'll never forget seeing a gallberry bush in a place of honor beside the lake in Callaway Gardens and having Fred Galle, then director of horticulture, identify it as an inkberry bush. "Gallberry!" I contradicted. "Ain't nothing but a gallberry!" He smiled and agreed that it had that common name, too. And then he pointed to its shiny black berries and finely cut green leaves. It was the first time I had ever looked at the gallberry for beauty instead of utility.

Well, it is a pretty little shrub, I can see that now, even while I check its branches for their yard-sweeping ability. Gallberry branches are closely placed and pliable, just right for sweeping if you prepare them properly. Of course, you cut the gallberry bushes green, haul them home and place them in the sun to dry. When the leaves have turned brown and are ready to fall off you give them a hand by beating the bush against a fence or stump or something.

Free of leaves, the twiggy branches are now ready to be bound together for a broom. I suppose there are broommakers who bound the stalks with twine. The ones I knew used strings of rags tied together.

This gave color to the handle of the broom and also made it a little softer to the hand that grasped it.

All this I can manage if I can ever find time to stop and cut or break the makings. I have heard of North Georgians who used dogwood for brush brooms, but I wince to think of that. Cutting a dogwood tree for such plebeian use is like killing a mockingbird. It should never be done. But now gallberry bushes could be sacrificed, and spring is coming.

January 17, 1986

Old Days
Old Ways

*T*he terse little note she handed me said, "Dr. Thomas Flaganan stopped by. Wants copy paper." I stood a minute puzzling over it and then I looked up and my young colleague was puzzled also but for a different reason. "What's copy paper?" she asked.

"What's COPY PAPER?" I cried. Then I subsided and offered her a rough idea. But the question stayed with me. "What's copy paper?" Oh, me, to think of that question being asked in a newspaper office! It shows how far we've come with computers and scanners and IBM Selectrix II. We use long sheets of slick white paper now, if we use paper at all. Most people write directly into machines in which their words rise up and rebuke them from a television screen.

Paper in a newspaper office may someday become as obsolete as Zinjanthropus.

But I remember it as vital as blood and bones and skin. Reporters did not use notebooks when I was young. A notebook for some reason was considered tacky and unprofessional. If you were a pro you had a wad of eight or ten sheets of copy paper folded just so and you took your notes on that. Skillful reporters knew how to fold their copy paper so their notes were down in sequence. I never learned that so there was an eternal battle to unscramble them back at the office. (Don't tell anybody but I was relieved when stenographer's notebooks became acceptable.)

Copy paper, of course, was cut from the nubbins left on the rolls of newsprint removed from the presses. Somebody went down to the press room and got it and sliced it into sheets — short ones for the copy desk to write heads on, longer ones for reporters' stories. They were sometimes lopsided as to shape and never long enough, those sheets of cream-colored, rough paper, so every desk had a glue pot on it. You glued your stories together. Sometimes the glue was good and binding. More often it soured and mildewed. Either way, your deathless prose, when set down on copy paper and looped together, had a distinctive smell to it.

There were other artifacts that went with copy paper. The black-leaded copy pencil, for one. I have friends, mostly crossword puzzle addicts, who will call me aside even today and in a conspiratorial whisper say, "Can you get ahold of some of those newspaper pencils for me?" I can't. I don't know where they went.

We are down to using pens now. Ink pens, as the school children used to specify. Notes you take with a black felt-tipped pen are certainly more legible than those taken in the copy pencil of yore — unless they get wet. Have you ever watched a neat black inky address wash off a letter on your way to the mail box?

❦ ❦ ❦

Then there was the copy spike. Stories written on newsprint and corrected in black copy pencil were then spiked on the city desk. Every desk had such a spike, weighted at the base with lead from the stereotype department.

The Occupational Safety and Health Administration came along and noted that these copy spikes could be lethal instruments. We all knew that. (I even wrote a murder mystery employing one.) But we didn't know anybody who was actually assaulted by one and some of us miss them today. The only two which survived the OSHA visit — and I have one of those — were bent to render them impotent.

Not knowing what copy paper was, today's young reporters can't join me in grieving for it. But it was good stuff — soft enough that you could dry hands on it or even use it for a handkerchief in a pinch. I even knew a successful novelist, an old newspaperman, who couldn't get to work on a new book until some of us found some copy paper for him.

Maybe that's what Dr. Flaganan had in mind when he came a-calling. But I can't help him now. I haven't seen any copy paper in years. Sob, sob.

May 16, 1980

*A*h, what a place it was—and how Atlantans loved it! Mooney's Lake, that is.

Since I attempted to answer an inquiry about the loveliest of all swimming holes here last week, the mail has flowed in like sweet clear artesian water from Mooney's Lake lovers all over Georgia and in neighboring states.

I have spoken with one of founder Deuward S. Mooney's two daughters, Estelle Mooney West Rives, who is spending the summer at Lakemont. I have heard from founder Mooney's grandson, who operates Hal West Real Estate at Clayton. I have talked with a man who saw Eugene Talmadge, Senator Herman Talmadge's father, taking a swim there when he was Commissioner of Agriculture and getting ready to run for governor.

Clippings have showered in from other writers who raised the "Where Was Mooney's Lake?" question, including a delightful one by William Hedgepeth writing for *Brown's Guide*. And the recollections—oh, my, the happy memories of hours spent there!

To get to the facts, Mrs. Rives and her son and historian Franklin Garrett told me that Deuward Mooney was a contractor, specializing in roofing, when he bought a lovely swatch of acreage out in the woods off Piedmont Road.

"It was country, nothing but country," said Mrs. Rives, who with her sister Leone, started life out as city girls, living on 12th Street. "The artesian water was beautiful, clear and cold, and he built us a pool first. And then—well, it attracted so many people it soon became an amusement park."

Franklin Garrett was a teen-age boy in the 1920s and he remembers Mooney's Lake as the only local lake with a cable ride. North of Peachtree Creek but in the Peachtree Creek valley, the lake had a small frame bathhouse after a while and then Mr. Mooney built a pavilion where food and drinks were available and there was a dance floor and jukebox and tables and benches overlooking the swimming pool.

Mrs. Rives and her son did not say but historian Garrett's records show that Mr. Mooney arrived in Atlanta about 1906. From that time until he moved to "the country" in 1919 he lived at 50 East 12th St. on the north side of the street between Juniper and Piedmont. Their lakeside home was made of Stone Mountain granite. "If my memory serves me correctly he was a man of small stature," says Garrett.

"He usually wore a black hat and had a sizable moustache. His transportation was a pickup truck which always rattled with tools and roofing materials.

❦ ❦ ❦

The Garretts lived on 13th Street from 1914 to 1921, and Mr. Garrett thinks he attended the old Tenth Street School, now no longer in existence, with Leone and Estelle.

Irene H. Barron was one of many recalling happy hours at the lake and she raised a new question. What happened to the little coal-fired train which started out in Piedmont Park, was in service at Mooney's Lake for a time and then disappeared?

"I would love to know what happened to it," she wrote. "It was an exact replica of a big steam engine."

The family did not mention the train but there was another mode of transportation which Hal West remembers with nostalgia. It was his. He was nine years old and he drove a billy goat wagon "full of roasted bagged peanuts for sale."

September 22, 1980

*N*ow I didn't go to make that mistake about the record-breaking drought of more than fifty years ago, but, boy, am I glad I made it. Otherwise, I wouldn't have heard from Joe Almand and I would have missed a marvelous session of reminiscence about the old days in north Fulton and south Milton counties.

It was not 1924 but 1925 that the Chattahoochee River slowed down to a trickle and women and small children were walking across it without wetting their skirts and coattails, said Mr. Almand. He should know. He was a teen-ager then, living on a farm on the river where the present Martin's Landing is.

"My mother's people, the Martins, came down from Fannin County in a covered wagon, driving two oxen, and settled there in old Milton County," Mr. Almand, now seventy-one years old, remembered. "My grandfather was A.A. Martin, a farmer, past grand master of the Masons and a justice of the peace who wore a claw-hammer coat when he dressed up.

"I'll never forget that summer. Heat? It was awful, it was terrible! We boys always spent a lot of time in the Chattahoochee. We knew that river like a muskrat would know it. But that summer we practically lived in it. To show you how bad that summer was, we planted cotton in April and our tracks were still in the field on the Fourth of July. No rain to spoil the tracks out!"

The Martins and the Almands had one stroke of luck. Crops were burned to a crisp all around them. Even gigantic hickory trees in the woods were dying and turning brown. Nobody had watermelons in watermelon season, of course, but they did. They had cleared some bottom land of briars and alders and planted the melons there. There was enough moisture in the soil to sustain them and when the Fourth of July, traditional watermelon-cutting day in the South, came, the family had them to sell in Roswell.

"Stone Mountain melons, they were called," Mr. Almand remembered. "Developed, I think, by Hastings and a fine, sweet melon but too brittle to ship. We had ice some of the time—a 300-pound block, bought in Roswell for ninety cents and packed in sawdust to keep it. We put ice in our milk and made ice cream on Saturday or Sunday but we didn't know anything about icing watermelons. Just put them under the beds in the house where it was dim and cool and they tasted just right when we cut them!"

Heat and drought weren't the only whims of nature to harass the Almands. The opposite, rainstorms and the flooding of the old Chattahoochee could be as bad. It was in the days before the Buford dam and its flood control propensity and the river overflowed its banks when a freshet hit it. One summer it overflowed the family's prime cottonfield, catching the cotton in the boll.

"There was a gin in Norcross that could handle it in the boll and we hitched up the wagon and took the cotton there," said Mr. Almand. "The cotton was kind of green, not first quality, and you know what we got for it? Three and a quarter cents a pound!"

🍎 🍎 🍎

The total pay for the family's labor in the field came to seventeen dollars. What did they do with it?

"I know exactly. We paid the guano bill we owed a Mr. Gantt who ran a warehouse in Norcross."

None left over for a treat for the children? Not that year, but Grandpa Martin had other irons in the fire. He was a professional syrup maker who ground sugar cane and made syrup for his family's use and for neighboring farmers. When harvest time and school starting loomed, the children were looked after.

"Went into the Roswell commissary and brought each of us a pair of Nunnally overalls for seventy-eight cents apiece," said Mr. Almand, laughing.

A citizen of DeKalb County since 1930, Mr. Almand still operates the textile bag business which brought him to the city fifty years ago. But he remembers well his childhood days at "Lizard Lope" on the Chattahoochee and his Powers ancestors' old place, "Ball Sluice," what is now called Morgan Falls. And every time I pass Lebanon church I'll remember that he was baptized there in a dammed-up creek where the shopping center is now.

July 20, 1981

*J*oyce Ojala, director of volunteer services at Grady Hospital, asked me to come down there for a meeting next week and then she very graciously sent me directions for finding her and the meeting when I arrive at the old hospital. Finding some given spot inside the hospital is, of course, far different from finding the hospital itself, but after I had read her note I sat long moments musing over it. Law me, child, I thought to myself, I bet I was puttering around what we lovingly call "the Gradys" before you were born!

There are plenty of people in Atlanta who have known Grady Hospital longer than I have. It has long since celebrated its hundredth birthday. But I don't know even native Atlantans who have known it more intimately. I have ridden its ambulances on Saturday night, sat up in its emergency room from sunset to sunrise, put in days hanging around its halls awaiting word on the condition of some famous citizen like Margaret Mitchell, taken my own emergencies there and stood by while countless Atlantans did the same.

I have been there with shooting victims. I was there when grieving parents went down to its morgue to try to identify their children who were burned beyond recognition in the Winecoff Hotel fire. I was there, gowned and masked, the summer a special ward filled up with polio patients. I hung around the office of Dr. William A. Friedewald when all of us hoped he was going to discover the cause and cure of the common cold at any moment.

Psychiatry, a brand-new, sort of voodoo exercise to me, entered my life at Grady when they invited me to sit in on some group therapy sessions. (Could it be possible, I wondered in amazement, that just sitting there *talking* would help those people? I think it did.)

Pete Landers, the policeman on duty in the emergency room, was a good friend of mine. Eunice Landers, secretary to the then superintendent, Frank Wilson, was a light unto my path when I stumbled around the old "Gradys" on stories. Margaret Stovall, my neighbor and former colleague at *The Constitution,* introduced me to many kind-hearted people who worked with her in the volunteer program there, including the late "Papa Sunshine," the merchant who never forgot his poverty-stricken early years and gave bountifully to Atlanta's less fortunate children.

It seems to me that Grady Hospital has drawn to its service some amazingly able and otherwise very busy people. I think often of Hughes Spalding, for whom the Spalding Pavilion was named, and the hours that he put in at the hospital, which in those days was a decrepit old Victorian residence with rickety additions spreading out beside it and behind it.

He was chairman of the Fulton-DeKalb Hospital Authority and one of the moving spirits behind what a lot of us will ever think of as "the new Grady." (Could it be that "the new Grady" is already old?) The old spiritual "Nobody Knows the Trouble I've Seen" might well be Grady's theme song. Every kind of trouble known to erring human beings winds up there.

The hospital itself has had touch-and-go financial problems. But some of us love it as we love our own families — its smells and crowds and Saturday night cries of pain, its compassion and caring, its eternal quest for answers and panaceas, its blessed humanity.

I haven't checked lately to see if the old magnolia tree in the front yard of the old Grady still talks. It used to have a speaker hidden somewhere in its leafy recesses that called doctors who might be crossing the street or moving about in other buildings and were needed back in the main building. I haven't "adopted" a child at Grady in many years but there was a time when I couldn't tear myself away from the little ones in the old children's ward.

Find the Gradys? I hope the day will never come when its comforting old silhouette doesn't stand like a rock on the Atlanta skyline.

November 2, 1982

*W*e wouldn't have believed it that summer of 1948, those of us who crowded into Judge Sam Boykin's courtroom in Coweta County courthouse. We wouldn't have believed that thirty-four years later people who weren't even born then would be reading a best-selling book and seeing an exciting movie about the odd crew of our fellow citizens we had come to know pretty well in the long hot days of the trial. John Wallace. Sheriff Lamar Potts. Miss Mayhayley Lancaster. The shy, scary girl whose sharecropper husband, William Turner, had been killed.

It was murder in Coweta County, all right. But we hadn't put it in capital letters. It remained for Margaret Anne Barnes, a writer, and the producers of the movie to call it "Murder in Coweta County." We should have known it was going to be an unforgettable story. I have spent thirty-four years remembering it. I covered some of the search for the body of the gaunt, overall-clad farm hand Turner. Photographer Floyd Jillson and I spent a day tracking down his wife and child, who had fled the county out of fear of John Wallace. I covered all the trial, which ran into two weeks. And I claimed the distinction of having "discovered" Miss Mayhayley Lancaster — the fortuneteller who figured in the trial and was one of the strangest, most fascinating characters I ever interviewed — remaining in touch with her until her death.

There have been a lot of murder trials and all of them stick in your mind in funny little bits and pieces. Sometimes it is the irrelevancies you remember far better than indictment, sentence or the judge's name. This is almost true of the trial of John Wallace. I remember the atmosphere in the courtroom, the crowds, the heat, Judge Boykin's disciplined handling of it all, particularly the press, which was limited to about three or four of us in those days.

I remember the witness who saw Wallace and his helpers run down and haul Turner out of the Sunset Tourist Camp and to his death. "What did you do when you saw that?" he was asked. "I went on eating," he said. I remember the efforts of an arrogant defense attorney, retained as an expert of toxicology, to break down the testimony of mild Dr. Herman Jones, director of the State Crime Lab, who was firm in his contention that a matchbox full of charred bones constituted the corpus delicti. Defense attorney Al Henson had bragged to me about his "expert," but when, after long, tedious, exhausting cross-examination, the visiting attorney, a very pompous fellow, had been unable to shake Dr. Jones, he shrugged in disgust. "When you see a feller who says 'supine' when he means 'laying down,' " said Mr. Henson, "you can put it down that he's a damned fool!"

❦ ❦ ❦

But best of all I remember the long ordeal of listening to Wallace make his unsworn statement. He began in a folksy, ingratiating tone, laying on one unimportant, uninteresting detail after another. But he came to the part where he and his cohorts had taken Turner to an abandoned well at gunpoint and held him poised there on the brink.

"I looked in the well. I looked in the well and I looked at Turner," Wallace said. "Turner said, 'Mister John, put me in that well and let me stay three or four hours. Then let me out of there and I'll move back here and help you find your cows.' "

Wallace said he heard a noise and he turned away. When he looked again, the gun in his hand had gone off.

"It was a bad dream," he said.

Two years and five appeals later, I talked to Wallace in Fulton Tower and he told me he had two reasons for knowing he would not die in the electric chair. Miss Mayhayley had said he'd live to be eight-eight years old. God said, "Whatsoever ye shall ask in prayer . . ."

But, of course, Wallace was electrocuted. He knelt and prayed in front of Reidsville's ugly old chair and Warden R.P. Balkcom Jr. told us all he had never "seen a man go to his death in such good spirits."

February 14, 1983

*I*magine my shock the other day to read a story from the Georgia Poison Control Center to the effect that applying meat tenderizer to an insect bite is "folk medicine." And all these years that I've been dusting mine and the children's itching, swelling bites with that stuff from the pantry shelf I thought it was the latest scientific wrinkle in the treatment of allergies. My idea of folk medicine was the old remedy — applying a wad of wet snuff or tobacco to the bite.

It just shows you that anything easy is unscientific. I've seen workmen slap mud on mosquito or yellow jacket bites and instead of dying from infection they apparently got immediate relief. The old granny woman who used to treat cuts with moldy bread had probably discovered penicillin and didn't know it. It was easy and it mostly worked — and what else was a poor country woman to do in the days when medical care and drugstores were far, far away?

The good thing about the Georgia Poison Control Center and Dr. Albert Rauber is that they didn't belittle the use of handy, at-home remedies so long as they work. They may be folk lore stuff but apparently they are respectable to the medical profession.

That's a good thing and I hope the experts pursue it further and let us know if sugar and Octagon soup, mashed and blended and held on with a clean white rag will "draw the poison" out of a rising and make it come to a head. (By the way, what whatever happened to "risings?" I haven't heard of one in years, even under their more common name, boils.)

I'd like to know if washing poison ivy welts with copperas water does any good and if sore throats derive any healing from a syrup made of sugar and stewed onions. All these hideous nostrums were used on me when I was a child because somebody was always telling my mother they were efficacious. An adventuresome spirit, she would try anything once, especially on me. The advocates of castor oil, salts, a patent medicine called Black Draught and similar purgatives had an eager disciple in my mother. I don't know how modern medicine feels about that spring purge when the system of man and beast (not to mention women and children) was commonly believed to need cleansing but I think some high crimes were committed in its name. Does anybody remember quinine for malaria and calomel for heaven knows what symptoms?

We didn't go in for dandelion greens in south Alabama and I don't remember that we even tried poke sallet, the standby of north Georgians. But we ate a lot of mustard greens, wilted in bacon drippings and seasoned with a dollop of vinegar so we must have achieved some kind of green help from the earth for weathering the hot days and nights when they came.

🍒 🍒 🍒

The efficacy of honey and vinegar was not known to me until years after I moved to Atlanta and read a book called "Folk Medicine." I tried it but I didn't notice any appreciable brightening of the eye or quickening of the step. Homemade jelly and hot biscuits are not the same, I am sure, but they seemed a happier way to greet the day.

The insidious thing about folk medicine is that it is more interesting, as well as cheaper, than more scientific remedies. Everybody has a favorite treatment, I am sure, the kind they practice in secret and can be persuaded to share only in the greatest secrecy. You feel like such a fool telling somebody that billy goat horns, soaked for ten days in May rainwater, result in a splendid tonic. So you practice your folk medicine in private and seldom, if ever, tell anybody.

Fortunately, my favorite home remedy is so well known that I have been able to go public with it. Everybody my age and many people far, far younger know that there's no treatment of the stubborn mean old chest cold like a flannel cloth fried in suet and turpentine. (I think. Or was it kerosene?) Fried clothes, as my mother called them, were miserable to sleep in but the fumes rising from them did all that television commercials claim for their modern cold remedies when it came to providing a night's rest.

Fried clothes I believe in. But I must confess I don't pour turpentine on rusty nail wounds any more.

July 17, 1983

*T*here comes a time in every life, I suppose, when the things you have promised to do and the things you have to do don't exactly mesh. You wake up in the morning with the feeling that you are miles behind on your duties and commitments. You go to bed at night wondering how you dare to close your eyes. The ogres of the undone or unfinished may come out of the woodwork and eat you up.

In such a state I came into the office the other night — the first time darkness has caught me loose on Marietta Street since the night of Jimmy Carter's defeat. (Come to think about it, I was in Plains that night all night — and that's a far piece from Marietta Street.) But being at work downtown was for many years normal procedure and I was unprepared for the changes.

❦ ❦ ❦

For one thing, our town looks beautiful at night, towers of building lights, cubes and pillars and cupolas, luminous and lambent. I had forgotten there were so many tall buildings and that they were so bright against the darkness. The expressways were garlands of automobile lights like the chains on a Christmas tree, the quiet streets shafts of radiance. There was almost no foot traffic and very little automobile traffic. A few cars moved lazily, slowly through the quiet business section, a lonely pedestrian or two walked toward the Five Points MARTA station. Buses lumbered up to intersections collecting a few late travelers.

I looked at my watch. It was not yet eight o'clock. Where did they go, all the people? I wondered. Time was when restaurants and hotels and movie theaters drew lively throngs to these streets. When you crossed Marietta Street in the early evening you were in the midst of a jostling crowd. The smell of food was rich in the air. Doors along Forsyth Street opened letting out the malty fragrance of beer and sometimes a patron or two who had been "waiting out the traffic" before starting home. Music poured out of night clubs upstairs over stores. You could hear the click of billard balls from pool halls. I missed another sound and I stood still in the middle of the sidewalk trying to define it.

The voices of the ragtag crew of newsies who peddled our newspaper. They hit the streets with the first edition and their raucous voices calling the headlines were the voices of the city. They carried the papers in all kinds of ways — bunched up in bags on their hips, in bicycle baskets and little red wagons — and even if the news was quiet, they weren't. They gave it an urgent ring making a little indictment, a small fraud, sound like war declared.

They are gone and in their places neat metal boxes, silent and chilly, let you have your paper if you have the change and persevere. They don't urge, insist, entice.

❦ ❦ ❦

Police cars and fire trucks and ambulances seem to hold their peace downtown these nights. When No. 1 Station was on Alabama Street its trucks' wild caterwauling in the night was a heart-stopping city sound. The clangor from the railroad yard, trains arriving and departing, switch engines jolting, coupling and uncoupling the big cars, was the background music for the drama of our town's night life.

What happened? Where did it all go? I miss Mrs. Arizona Bell hawking her papers at the corner of Walton and Broad, Icky and his girlfriend barking at one another across Marietta Street in a kind of newsie's love call. I miss the sound of the professor's violin in the old Victorian building that stood at the corner of Marietta and Forsyth and drew him music students until late hours of the night. I miss Western Union as it used to be, a vast office with marble counters and frenzied goings and comings.

It certainly seems peaceful, this new downtown — and safe. And lonesome. I felt strange to be loose in it after dark and I must have looked strange. There was quite a delay getting past the security guard and into our building.

February 19, 1984

*R*eg Murphy, our former editor, now publisher of the *Baltimore Sun,* spoke to the Atlanta Press Club the other day and said laughter and levity have all but vanished from the political scene. He didn't place any blame, but the tenor of his remarks suggested that the press has lost its sense of humor and, if a politician opens his mouth and says something funny, we're prone to make him look like an idiot before the electorate.

In a word, we don't savor our satirists and our cutups the way we once did. And a politician who tries to amuse may get ridicule instead of appreciation.

There has long been a theory that newspaper people don't have the fun and games the job once included. I don't know if this is true because I'm not hanging around the office after hours when the paper has been put to bed and the fellows relax and indulge in foolishness. I do know that I miss a lot of the intramural jokes that once kept us laughing. There was Harold Martin, as hard-working a reporter and as gifted a writer as ever lived. And as full of pranks as a kid. I shared an office with him, but I never got used to opening my desk drawer and climbing the wall in screeching terror because he had thoughtfully placed a coiled, lifelike plaster snake in there. This is to justify the sign he brought back from some Florida roadside emporium reading "STOP! GAS! SEE BIG SNAKE!" That sign ornamented our office door for years.

At the end of a long stint of hard work, when he finished a piece for the *Saturday Evening Post,* Harold was prone to lift his voice in song, leading our end of the hall in "Amazing Grace" and "May the Circle Be Unbroken." My lifelong habit of kicking off my shoes when I sit down played right into my roommate's hands. When I got engrossed in a story, he would pass my desk looking innocent and businesslike. And my shoes would be gone. Late one afternoon, he went home without telling me where my shoes were, and I got sent out to cover a fire — in my stocking feet.

Old *Atlanta Georgian* hands remembered well the day Harold slipped a man with a big black bear on a leash up the back elevator and into the newsroom and set them to reading copy over City Editor Charlie Shonesey's shoulder. I'd like to have been there when Charlie, a fire-eating city editor of legend, glanced up and saw the bear. The shock practically reduced the newsroom to rubble, and Charlie was subdued to the point of voicelessness for three days.

Even Ralph McGill, the serious-minded editor, broke down and pulled memorable pranks now and then.

Pint-sized Lee Fuhrman, war-time city editor of *The Constitution,* spread his humor around. When schoolchildren approached the office on tour, he grabbed an eyeshade for his brow and three telephones for props and started yelling, "Get me Joe Stalin on the phone! Get me Eleanor Roosevelt!" The men reporters loyally stuck press cards in their hat bands and let cigarettes hang out the corners of their mouths.

For years, we couldn't tell anybody about the New Year's Eve when Davison's time telephone line and one of our sports department lines got crossed. Lee learned that everybody in town was calling the time number to check the approach of midnight, and the answer was a litany: "Take your chargaplate and — it! This is Davison's, eelevun forty-ninuh." Or "Your chargaplate ain't worth a damn. This is Davison's, ee-leven-fifty-two!" The next day Davison's was swamped with complaints. After Lee had died, and just before my friend Rosalind Williams, Davison's advertising manager, went to France and died in the Orly plane crash, I told her what had happened. She didn't laugh even then, but some of us do when we remember. That's the trouble about humor. There's no guarantee it is funny to everybody.

January 30, 1987

*T*he theme of going home again is pretty general in almost all books, I suppose. Thomas Wolfe certainly didn't invent it for "You Can't Go Home Again" because thousands of writers before him and since him have delved poignantly into the feelings of characters who try to return to scenes of the past, usually well-loved ones, and wistfully and plaintively discover they aren't there anymore.

The other day, my son and his wife took a step on the journey toward our old home — the spot where he grew up and where we lived for almost two decades, 13th Street between the Peachtrees. I had told them about the beautiful IBM building on West Peachtree two blocks from our old house, and they had admired it as the most graceful tower on Atlanta's skyline. I knew an office where they might let us in to look out the window, I told them, and then we found an even better deal — the beautiful, big untenanted fiftieth floor. It is not open to the public, someone told me, because workmen are still busy there trying to put it in shape for new tenants. But we took a chance that they would let us in for a few minutes to look down on the days of yesteryear, and they did.

❦ ❦ ❦

Somehow it makes me sad to look down on the roof of a new office building on the very ground where I planted zinnias, where my children had their sandbox, where we picked up sweetgum balls and gilded them for Christmas. I yearned for the dark lines of the old roof that sheltered us all those years, for the alley through which a little creek with banks of bluets ran in rainy weather. I reviewed the roll of old neighbors who bought carnival tickets and Girl Scout cookies and gave me cuttings of tea olive to try to root. I grieved that I had lost touch and wondered if the nice couple who shared our big orange cat with us, each of us supposing we were the sole owner, still live.

My son, on the other hand, had a perfectly marvelous time "going back." The towering ceilings of the IBM lobby, the elegant marble everywhere delighted him, and he kept wishing Mr. Giles, who ran a grocery store on that spot, could be there to see it. He didn't grieve for Hawks' drugstore across the street, but marveled instead at the novelty of seeing a bright green lawn growing there instead of the racks of comic books where as a little boy, he was wont to freeload.

❦ ❦ ❦

Once Dr. Hawks offended him mightily by suggesting that he drank the drugstore's ice water free and read the comic books as fast as they came in, seldom buying. Later, our neighborhood druggist reported to me that my son had drawn himself up proudly and stalked out saying, "I'll take my business elsewhere."

Now he lives elsewhere and remembers with the greatest affection that place and those people. And looking down on the spot where they used to be from the big windows of a mighty skyscraper filled him with pleasure.

"Look!" he cried. "there's Mrs. Garmon's house — still there! And Mrs. Baldwin's and Mrs. Rush's. See where that blue car is, I left my bicycle there one day and somebody ran over it."

"Over there," I offered, going to another window, "where that motel is, there was a big clay hill. You all called it Mud Mountain and ruined your clothes sliding on it."

He held out a hand. "I've still got a scar on this finger from something I cut it on over on Mud Mountain."

We looked at the expressway pulsing with traffic and remembered when it was woods before the big bulldozers and other earthmovers moved in. We hadn't known what an expressway was but, looking back, I wonder if we didn't think it was kind of an honor having it come into our neighborhood, something like being, I know now, being a city important enough to be bombed in wartime.

March 6, 1989

*T*t's very hard to walk around downtown Atlanta now. The tearing down and rebuilding must have been an Atlanta trademark since the first returning householder after Sherman's big fire found a few boards and nailed them together. But I think the process has been stepped up.

That may be because landmarks I knew have tottered and fallen and been crushed and hauled away. It's not just our restless city's style any more. It's personal. I don't mind taking my chances in the street around "Sidewalk Closed" signs. I'm used to that. I don't mind those ghostly sheets of fabric they use to swathe building projects flapping in my face. I know they are there to save us pedestrians from fallout.

What I do mind is looking at a big hole in the ground and realizing that's where the Ansley Hotel stood—just the other day, it seems.

It's not that I had any particular affection for that old hotel. Other, grander hotels have come and gone. Remember the Kimball House? It was an architectural gem, which would be reverently preserved now. Remember the Piedmont, with its Oak Room and unsurpassed roast beef? Remember the Biltmore and the Georgian Terrace, where we went to interview opera singers and movie stars, and the Henry Grady, the political center of the state, which also had space for such visitors as Carson McCullers, Eleanor Roosevelt and Vladimir Horowitz?

They have had their day and that day has passed and I'm reconciled, but I had to stop a few moments by that muddy hole up on Forsyth Street and think about the old Ansley. It's true it lost its identity years ago when the Dinkler family bought and renamed it. Even then, as a hotel, it did not survive. But I didn't realize that it was really gone until I saw that hole in the ground.

While the Henry Grady got most of the politicians, a few chose the Ansley for their campaign headquarters and, of course, the scene of election night celebrations. I stood there thinking of the winners and the losers I had interviewed there, of the theater in the round that once flourished on the Ansley roof. The old actress, Georgia Simmons, who later came home to Georgia to die, starred there with John Carradine in "Tobacco Road." She was a memorable Ada and he was the best Jeeter Lester this side of James Barton and Broadway.

❦ ❦ ❦

There was a place to eat in the basement called the Owl Room, where many convivial parties assembled. Civic clubs held their luncheons there and celebrities were guests there. My editor friend, the beautiful auburn-haired Isabelle Taylor of Doubleday, did not get there until the Ansley had been bought by the Dinkler family and had its name changed. I don't think the name change caught Mrs. Taylor's attention until she had checked in and gone to the bathroom. There before the toilet was a bathmat with the words "The Dinkler" emblazoned on it.

Mrs. Taylor gave way to a fit of the giggles.

"It said 'The Dinkler,' " she chortled. "I *knew* what it was!"

As a gesture of good will, Nancy McLarty, the hotel's public relations person, presented Mrs. Taylor with a bathmat as a keepsake.

It occurred to me as I stood by the hole that I should call out to a man on a bulldozer to learn what they're planning to build there. But instead I picked my way down the muddy side street to Fairlie, where there was also a sidewalk obstruction detour, and on down to Cone, where something is being hammered and drilled to replace the Old Georgia Hotel. No use to ask for whom the bulldozer growls, I muttered, paraphrasing John Donne. If you live in Atlanta, it growls for thee.

November 20, 1989

Portrait Gallery

*H*is name is Bill, a good name he has handed down to a son and a grandson. We call him Mister Willie out of fun and affection. Her name is Secessia, after an old friend of her mother's who was born in those crucial days of 1860, when Louisiana and her sister Southern states seceded from the Union. They will be celebrating their sixtieth wedding anniversary next week. The invitation to a gala party for two hundred relatives and friends said, "No gifts, please."

Since the invitation has been thumbtacked to the bulletin board in my kitchen I have thought a lot about them and the question of gifts. It would be very difficult to decide on a gift for them, material or spiritual. When you have been keeping house since 1922 it isn't likely that you need anything that you haven't already acquired for comfort or convenience. In fact, the pattern seems to run the other way, I notice. You begin to divest yourself of things.

The really good gifts they have had in abundance. He was a railroad man in an era when railroading was perhaps a more exciting field than aviation ever became. She was a nurse, who lived close to life and death and had the sure knowledge that she helped, really helped, people. They reared two terrible worrisome, aggressive sons, who must have kept them seesawing between tears and laughter for years before they settled down to being highly successful businessmen, estimable citizens and, best of all, fathers and grandfathers of many more children.

❧ ❧ ❧

I think often of the time Bill Jr. decided to provide the table with a Christmas goose, which he would illegally shoot over Lake Pontchartrain. He got his goose and was pedaling swiftly and furtively home with it lashed to his bicycle, certain the game warden was after him, when a woman motorist hit him. Her wheel struck boy and goose and bike—but mostly goose. She was too hysterical to see that the goose was the source of the blood and guts—and Billy was in too big a hurry to leave the scene to reassure her. What I've never checked is how his otherwise calm parents weathered the bloody, mangled spectacle of boy, bike and goose.

It was to Sech and Mister Willie perhaps a minor commotion in a life filled with them. They nursed the old people in their families, and assorted nieces and nephews on both sides were as much concern to them as their own children. They had troubles, as all families do, and weathered the lean days of the Depression with more humor than meal in the bin.

❦ ❦ ❦

And ah, the successes they have had—the loving grandchildren and great grandchildren who fill their white small frame house in Metairie with noise and laughter, long-time friends and neighbors who will gather to fete them, sisters and brothers and nieces and nephews who remember gifts and opportunities they provided. They have rich memories. Their grandson, the third Bill, now a doctor in Texas, earned his first spending money picking and selling figs from the tree in their backyard. I think of this Bill and his little-boy outrage when some member of the family died and he was not allowed to make the trip from Houston to New Orleans for the funeral.

"I tell you one thing," he warned his parents, looking at his beloved grandfather, Mister Willie, "when Granddaddy dies I'm going to his funeral!"

Mister Willie cocked an appreciative eye at his grandson and said jauntily, "Don't rush me, son, don't rush me!"

It's the last thing the family and friends of Mister Willie and Sech want to do— rush them. They will want them to have a happy 60th wedding anniversary and many more. I know some of them will disobey the no-gifts rule and go laden with presents. I can't think what, because actually they've had it all.

November 12, 1982

*O*ur friend Mac McKay died the morning after Christmas and although we had been expecting it, the finality of his death was a painful blow to us and, I realized even as I wiped my own tears away, to literally hundreds of other people. For Mac (his proper name was Richard) was a life-saver. For the past eight or ten years he had devoted himself to salvaging the lives of that singularly unlovable group of people: Drunks.

The smelly, boring, destructive alcoholic you might think the Lord Himself finds trying and unattractive, was to Mac McKay somebody worth saving and he went out of his way to help them. At all hours of the night and day he was on call when somebody he knew or even a rank stranger, wearying of a messy and wasted life, cried out for help. He went to their homes. He brought many of them into his own home, where he plied them with food and coffee and oftentimes hot baths and clean clothes. He believed in the spark that many of us think has been snuffed out in the heart and soul of drunks we know. He believed it could be rekindled and through his devotion and that of others with whom he worked, it often was.

Mac himself had been an alcoholic. Since I have known him he has been, as he himself put it, "non-practicing," instead of reformed or cured. It was his theory that if you're once an alcoholic you are always an alcoholic and the thing that counted was whether you practiced sobriety or didn't. He found sobriety in his own life a kind of awesome miracle that made him want to share it with others and share he did. He was particularly concerned about teen-agers and went into high schools to talk to groups.

Once, I heard him relate, with a lump in his throat, that when he went to his granddaughter's school he told her ahead of time that he was appearing anonymously and he did not want to embarrass her by letting her classmates know that he was her grandfather. The little girl threw him a surprised look, walked up to him before all her friends and said clearly, "This is my grandfather." To him she whispered, "I'm proud of you!"

It was one of the happiest moments of his life and one he would have liked to have seen duplicated in the lives of men and women who through alcoholism have lost their own wives and husbands, children and grandchildren.

The son of a Congregational minister, Mac was a member of a big family and he considered his own family a totally satisfying blessing. When he went to the hospital he insisted on taking their pictures with him. When he worked around the house — and he was both a gifted gardener and landscape architect — he delighted in the presence of tree-climbing, wheelbarrow-pushing youngsters.

Although he had a notable World War II experience, suffering disabilities in the jungles of the Philippines which were to dog him all his life, Mac seldom spoke of the war. When he did it was unforgettable. He was in the Air Force and his plane was shot down in an area which was held by the Japanese. One night two or three of us sat in his living room and heard him retell the details of a six-week walk to safety. It had been harrowing but Mac told it with some humor and a lot of self-deprecation. If he was a hero, he didn't mention it and it only struck me later that, of course, he was a hero. Not only in the fight for his country but in the bigger, more complicated, more difficult battle of living.

He will be sorely missed.

December 29, 1980

*A*radio interviewer was asking me about what they now call "role models" — a flossy term, I think, for a person who possesses all the qualities you admire, achieves the things you consider of value and generally constitutes your personal hero or heroine. It was easy for me to name one right off: Grace Towns Hamilton, for nearly twenty years a member of the Georgia House of Representatives.

It pleased me no end to learn a couple of days later that Emory University shares my high opinion of Mrs. Hamilton. It awarded her its honorary degree of Doctor of Laws with a citation which said:

"Distinguished lawmaker, beloved and honored citizen of Atlanta, through your personal and political influence you have played an important role in the emergence of the New South over the last four decades, first in encouraging and later in crafting landmark legislation. The legislative victories to which you have so formidably contributed track the maturing of our city and state; ensuring fair elections, more equitable political representation and employment opportunities, comprehensive regional planning, fair treatment of persons displaced by modernization, and state support of public and teaching hospitals, to name only a few."

Ah, I thought, Emory knows it all. It has been watching Grace all these years she has been hard at work over there at the Capitol, gently, courteously, quietly getting a better deal for the disfranchised, the homeless, the ill and infirm, plugging away at the problems of quality education for everybody. But I bet even the learned university doesn't know Grace the way I do.

Has it slogged through slums with her on a hot, airless day, visited pokey little health centers in black neighborhoods, listened to her, soft-voiced and smiling, persuade a group of stubborn, hard-headed men to her way of thinking at some boring committee or board meeting? Did the Emory degree-awarders ever sit in Grace's back yard on a hill overlooking Atlanta and see the love on her face when she looked out over the railroad tracks and factory buildings, the skyscrapers and the tenements, the big universities and the stores and churches and tired, dusty streets?

Mrs. Hamilton was the first black woman to serve in the Georgia General Assembly and she's been there longer than any other woman — called "the lady from Fulton" by her colleagues. She took up politics, she has often said, as her "retirement occupation" but it has really been a continuation of what she was doing when I first met her, working at the Atlanta Urban League for education, health and housing. She had an idea that better laws could prevent a lot of misery and inequity in all walks of life, and I think she has clung to it and worked for it even when there were discouraging and disillusioning days at the Capitol.

Perhaps I admire Grace Hamilton most because she loves Atlanta, as I do, but with a difference. She has done something about it. Born and educated here, she knows her town's faults as a mother knows her child's and she has seen it make some bad mistakes. But she also has seen its struggles, helped it to many of its successes, looking into its heart and believing in it all the time.

Sometimes, it has seemed to me that Grace Hamilton has the true humility only given to the well-born, the carefully reared, the well-educated. The daughter and wife of Atlanta University professors, and herself a teacher on occasion, she seems able to instruct people without pushing herself or raising her voice. And yet she has risen to a position of influence and leadership in the Georgia House, serving on the policy committee and as a member of the subcommittee on Human Resources, among others.

But I like best what the late Hughes Spalding, chairman of the Fulton DeKalb Hospital Authority, said of her: "You have to believe in Mrs. Hamilton. She gets her facts, she never goes off half-cocked, and she is *good*."

June 3, 1984

*T*he letter was written in red ink on the margin of a Colorado newspaper. Some of it was undecipherable. Some of it was pure Francis Brunton. I felt cheered and in touch by the message: "I'm going to have a good year. I saw the desert. Wishing you the same."

Of course, Francis Brunton is going to have a good year wherever he is, excusing being locked up. He mortally despises confinement. And if you think it's a non sequitur, "I'm going to have a good year. I saw the desert," think again. This is a rich and profound statement of Francis' philosophy. He has seen bleakness, emptiness, vast unfamiliar distances and he is shored up in his belief that he is going to have a good year.

To some of us, any year not spent on the desert will be a good year.

Maybe some of you are so new in town you don't remember Francis, a picturesque newsie, who sold our paper on the sidewalks of Atlanta for a time. Then he took up bike riding and wasn't seen so often hereabouts.

But if you saw him, you'd remember him.

His costume was memorable: puttees, baseball socks and shoes, a railroad engineer's cap and a full complement of maps and globes stung over his person. He packed his worldly goods in two Walgreen's shopping bags.

(Whatever happened to Walgreen's fine, sturdy shopping bags?) He was a small, slightly wizened man, terribly nearsighted, and he sported a rather frazzled beard back before beards were chic.

He was, as we say in the South, funny, which means a trifle askew in demeanor and behavior but by no means crazy. Eccentric, perhaps. Unusual, of course. But pleasantly so. He was a man of good humor and great will, and he is perfectly willing to endure the hardships of sleeping under the viaduct or in doorways to maintain his freedom from employment or economic fetters.

(Once I helped him get a job picking pimentos on a farm near Woodbury. A paycheck and a small apartment over the garage were included, and the work was not particularly hard. He despised it. It interfered with his freedom to bicycle here and there over the countryside, and it consumed time he preferred to spend reading. He quit.) So Francis didn't mind discomfort. He took his meals with whatever church was having a fellowship supper — and it seems that there's one of these almost every night in the week. Francis was welcome to most, if not all, of them. But some of the fancier specialty shops were prone to be a little sniffy about his appearance and perhaps the fact that he was unable to keep himself rose-petal fresh even with the bathroom facilities at his command. I remember one time he called me from Franklin Simon's pretty, flossy emporium out Peachtree Street.

He was just in there sort of looking around, he said, but somebody had called the police.

"What must I do?" he asked.

"Have they got a back door?" I inquired.

He said he saw one and I said, "Take it!"

He pedaled off into the sunset, a free man. He has managed to stay free most of the time. There was a time in Cloudland, Minnesota, but the doctor in charge of that mental hospital was a reasonable man and after a little time he released Francis to head west.

I hear from him now and then, and I'm always glad to know that he's loose in the world, enjoying himself, visiting libraries and collecting papers and books out of garbage cans.

He doesn't write detailed letters. Or rather I don't garner many details out of his letters. They sometimes run long, and occasionally they have a glimmering meaning for me. But that's not necessary. Francis values freedom of syntax as much as freedom of movement.

Nevertheless, the new year seems to me to begin auspiciously if I get a red-inky letter from my old friend. Maybe he will have a good year, having seen the desert. And wasn't it like him to wish us, his Atlanta friends, the same?

January 6, 1986

*H*is beautiful tenor voice is stilled. No longer will his scarlet satin cape swirl over the pews in Big Bethel A.M.E. Church as he leaps, pitchfork in hand, out to entice a new sinner to hell. No longer will countless Atlantans, tears in their eyes, get to their feet to follow his lead in singing, "Swing Low Sweet Chariot" and "Hand Me Down My Silver Trumpet Gabriel."

Henry J. Furlow, the world's most beguiling Satan, is dead. His funeral will be at Big Bethel, where he was a member and choir director for more than fifty years.

A member of the congregation called to tell me about Mr. Furlow's death, and I was sorry I hadn't known he was ill. He had been ill for some time, and I didn't get there to pay my respects to a fine teacher, a fine gentleman.

Almost every October that I've been in Atlanta, I have been in touch with Henry Furlow—at least since that first one many years ago when my late boss, Ralph McGill, urged me to go down on Auburn Avenue to see "Heaven Bound," the old allegory which has been played out there since 1930.

Henry Furlow, agile and graceful up into his seventies, was the flaming, villainous star of the story, but there were many stars. He and his wife, the church organist, directed them all. The story, written for the church by an old Sunday school teacher, is so simple and childlike as to be a classic on a par with "Pilgrim's Progress." It concerns the journey toward heaven of sinners, all kinds of sinners, such as the Wayward Girl, the Drunkard, the Gambler, the Rich Man, the Widow and the Orphans, the Soldier of the Lord and many more.

The church chancel and choir loft are always decorated like heaven with blue paper skies and white clouds, and there are pearly gates manned by a gray-bearded St. Peter in a golden crown.

Every time a sinner embarks on that last journey, the heavenly chorus—and Big Bethel's choir is heavenly—tries to sing him to glory. But the old devil is after him, too—flattering, cajoling, bribing—and the flames of hell await in his corner of the church.

There are new devils now, and I haven't seen them perform, but Mr. Furlow's performance could not be surpassed. He was an inspired actor and a wonderful singer, and he took great personal pleasure in the success of "Heaven Bound" each year. The original cast grew old and some members died. Sons and daughters took their places and then grandsons and granddaughters. The show went on every autumn and until three or four years ago, I would get a call or receive a visit from Mr. Furlow to remind me and usually to present me with a couple of tickets.

Quiet and soft-spoken, he never lingered long. He was a retired high school teacher, and occasionally he chatted a moment or two about the importance of bringing up children in strong faith and — he always smiled when he said this — the enjoyment of music. Music was important to him, an integral part of his daily life, and he gloried in the fact that Big Bethel choir, largely untrained when he started out, became one of the most famous choirs in the city. Its selection of music turned toward classical hymns as the years progressed, and the education of the singers improved, but on "Heaven Bound" night, you could always count on the singing of spirituals. "All Hail Immanuel" would be there and so would that spine-tingler, "Steal Away" and "I Was 'Way Down Yonder by Myself and I Couldn't Hear Nobody Pray."

Recently I read Coretta Scott King's fine biography of her husband, Martin Luther King Jr., and I was impressed to see how the old songs of his race had wrapped themselves 'round his heart, and he wanted to hear them again and again. Big Bethel and Ebenezer are neighbor churches, and members of both will probably be together to pay tribute to a man who earned a place for himself in the hearts of all Atlantans.

August 12, 1986

A lot of us called him "Willie," going back to the day thirty-three years ago when he walked into the old *Constitution* newsroom, in that now park-like niche next to Rich's, and began work as an editorial assistant to Editor Ralph McGill and Associate Editor Jack Tarver.

He was a skinny, black-eyed young fellow, lonely because his wife Hazel and their baby had not come up from Savannah to join him yet, and we all were pleased to include him in gatherings that the young people on the staff were having. He told us then that his job on *The Atlanta Constitution* was a fluke. Tarver and McGill had meant to hire the *Savannah Morning News'* star reporter, Bill Fielding.

Bill Fielding wasn't available, he told us, so *The Atlanta Constitution* got Bill Fields. It was an error nobody ever regretted.

He went on to become an important person in the newspaper's management. But he never acted important. His attitude, when they promoted him from editorial assistant to associate editor, prevailed all the years that he worked and advanced in the newspaper hierarchy.

The first promotion to associate editor was dazzling to us, his friends, and we gathered around to congratulate him.

He frowned at our exuberance and brushed aside our compliments.

"Aw, it's nothing," he said. "They just changed me from ed ass to ass ed."

Fields became executive editor of both *The Atlanta Constitution* and *The Atlanta Journal* and a vice president, but he wandered through the building every day, stopping to talk a moment or two with everybody who had the time. He knew when we had troubles, and he helped us with loans, advice and sympathy. He knew our children and asked about them. He visited our sick with us in hospitals, and he attended our weddings and funerals. He was keenly aware of our work, quick to point out shortcomings and slow, we all thought, to praise. But his praise was valued when it came.

For years, he heard me talking about the novel I intended to write, and occasionally, he nagged me to get on with it. One day, I found on my desk a hefty volume in which he had inscribed my name and these words: "This will tell you all you need to know about writing a novel. It cannot, however, use a typewriter."

❦ ❦ ❦

When I wrote about that, and *Reader's Digest* picked up the paragraph and sent me a hefty check for seventy-five dollars, I fleetingly considered that Fields was entitled to a cut. "No," he said gruffly. "Pay your telephone bill. I know it's past due." It was and I did. "Sibley owes me money," he liked to say.

I owed him a great deal more. We all did. None of us could believe that he died so unexpectedly, so swiftly as he did Saturday morning. We counted on his living forever, for being there when we needed him. Only ten days ago, he drove up from Savannah to check on a longtime staff member, who has been ill and in trouble. Willie looked great, we all told one another, clearly enjoying the retirement that freed him from us and our concerns.

But, of course, he wasn't free. Pretending cynicism, polishing up his acid comments, he was unable to deny the great reservoirs of concern, generosity, even love that welled up within him where his friends and co-workers were concerned.

Former *Constitution* Editor Gene Patterson once told me, when we drove down to Columbia, Alabama, to the funeral of Willie's mother, that you knew why he was a person of integrity, of great strength when you saw his beginnings in the little town and met his family. Today, when we go down to Savannah for his funeral, a lot of us will know the depths of his family's grief. We feel that we are family, too.

February 23, 1987

*S*he looked like a cherub or a kewpie doll, a plump little woman with bright dark eyes, silky dark eyebrows, a scarlet cupid's bow mouth and a head full of bouncing snow-white curls. She had a husky voice, a ready laugh and a heart as big as all outdoors. Her name was Blanche Matthews and she died last week at the age of seventy-four.

Blanche and I knew each other at Herren's restaurant, where she worked as a waitress for thirty-three years — until the day of her death, in fact — and lately as fellow passengers on the MARTA bus and train from Roswell. We talked almost daily about many things, but until her death, I wasn't really aware of the breadth and depth of her friendships, her kindness, her generosity.

The day of her funeral, I called Herren's to talk to her boss, Ed Negri. I got a recorded message. The restaurant was closed for the day in tribute to Blanche. At the same time, scores of prominent Atlantans, business and civic leaders and public officials were assembling for her funeral at Our Lady of Assumption Catholic Church.

"I think she knew everybody in town," Ed Negri was to say later. "She had a phenomenal memory and her regular customers were almost family to her. I don't believe anybody in my family or anybody that she knew ever had a hard day that they didn't receive a card or a note from Blanche. Often, if she thought it suitable, she stuck in a dollar. Her daughter, Connie [Mrs. James McTaggart] said, 'There are a lot of dollars out there.' I guess you could say Blanche was about as close to being a saint on earth as you've ever seen."

❧ ❧ ❧

A native of New York, Blanche was a member of a big, close family. She and her husband, Richard Ellison Matthews, an Air Force man, picked Atlanta as a home for themselves and their six children following his retirement from the service. Mr. Matthews had an automobile dealership until he was stricken with illness. Then Blanche went to work.

"If it was hard, we never knew it," said Connie. "I never heard her complain. And I never heard her say a critical or an unkind thing about anybody."

The only near-complaint that anybody drew from Blanche was with the suggestion that she stop work. She abhorred the idea, only consenting to cut down on her hours after she turned seventy.

"She loved going to town and being busy," Connie said.

Fourteen or fifteen years ago, I took my grandson Ted to Herren's after a movie at the Rialto to celebrate his eighth birthday. Blanche was our waitress, of course, but I don't remember telling her it was Ted's birthday.

Nevertheless, with dessert, she brought a cupcake bearing a lighted birthday candle. It is, Ed Negri said, a custom of the house if the waitress happens to know, but Blanche, a grandmother herself and very intuitive, did it more often than most.

Mr. Negri said of Blanche what an old friend said of her husband when he died after fifty years of marriage: "It's not enough." A lot of us feel that Blanche's death deprived us. But I think Blanche herself was ready for her death, even looking forward to it. She and her daughter, with whom she lived, were both wakeful on the night before she died, and they sat talking into the early hours of the morning. When Connie got sleepy, she crawled in bed with her mother and was dozing off when she felt Blanche sit up in bed.

"Honey, I'm not ready to go to sleep," Blanche said. Those were her last words and, thinking about it, Connie and I decided she knew death approached and she wanted to be awake and ready, her white curls bobbing, her bright eyes wide and watchful.

March 30, 1987

*S*everal years ago, I was making a book tour in North Carolina, and the young publisher's representative who was hauling me around asked me about Atlanta's famous Faith Brunson, book buyer at Rich's and president of the American Booksellers Association.

"One of my oldest friends," I said promptly. "Hardworking, outrageous, funny, Mississippi family-oriented and intensely loyal to her friends."

He was silent a moment.

"You know," he confessed after a time, "I thought she was a mean old lady with sharp, pointed teeth. I heard she ate book salesmen for breakfast."

"Well, she can be pretty fierce," I said when I could stop laughing. "But she has beautiful teeth. Regular, not pointed."

The young man pulled up in front of a bookstore where I was to autograph, and it looked peaceful and quiet to the point of desertion.

"I just wish I had a Faith Brunson in every state I cover," he said wistfully.

He was not alone in that wish. Faith, until Rich's cut her loose when it closed down its book operation under the recent new ownership, was one of the premier book sellers in the country. Although she battled with publishers' men from time to time when they tried to sell her titles she considered unworthy of Rich's, they respected and loved her. Proof of that was a gala reception that publishers, their salesmen and many of the authors Faith has boosted to best-sellerdom staged at the Atlanta Historical Society the other night.

Even Faith thought it was fun, and she would rather be selling books any day than talking about them. Some people, she freely admitted, have high-flown slogans to live by. Hers was simply the merchandiser's code: "Beat last year!" She publicly insisted that she sold, did not read, books. But we caught her in a fib there. Publishers often sent her manuscripts for her opinion. And as Betsy Fancher, longtime friend and author, once whispered to me, "I think Faith is a closet reader."

Mississippi contributed Faith to the book world. Her hometown, where a greatly loved cousin named Lolita still lives and makes fig preserves to be mailed to Atlanta, was Columbia. "Out from," Faith always specified.

Her love and loyalty for her employer knew no bounds. Once a best-selling minister got weary of autographing books and set his secretary to the task in Faith's office. When a customer, an old lady, paid for her "personally autographed" book, she showed Faith the flyleaf.

"Look at his handwriting," she said, running a reverent finger over the words, "Jesus loves you." "You can tell he's a holy man."

Faith looked at the inscription and realized the writing had changed somewhat. She dashed into her office and found the counterfeiting secretary at work.

"Stop it!" she yelled, and went in search of the minister-author. "You can be dishonest about your autograph if you want to. But Rich's doesn't lie! I'm not selling any more of your books with those fake autographs!"

Faith is as plain and outspoken about everything. Once I heard an affluent friend of ours reminiscing about her childhood days in Atlanta. She remembered fondly that "grandmother's chauffeur" had driven her to concerts and parties.

"Hmm," sniffed Faith. "While you were riding around behind 'grandmother's show-furr,' I was getting around south Mississippi on one skate."

Her parents, she contended, couldn't afford to buy a pair of skates for each of their two daughters so they bought one pair, which they divided. Her family stories are so good I often have urged her to write them. But then, her bons mots aren't bad. For instance, she once assured me that four-letter words didn't bother her. The ones she deplored, she said, were the three-letter ones: "O-l-d, a-g-e, f-a-t."

November 18, 1988

*T*he old John Donne line — "Any man's death diminishes me, because I am involved in mankind" — is often quoted, but it does not always seem as true to me as it did last week when I went to the funeral of an old country neighbor, "Miss Artie" Cox. The whole time I was sitting in the Alpharetta chapel listening to the songs and the funeral sermon about Miss Artie, I kept thinking how her going diminished, if not actually destroyed, the part of Sweet Apple settlement of happy recollection when it was still a country place, with farmer neighbors who had mules and kept cows and invited us to hog-killings.

Miss Artie had been so much a part of that time when I was new at Sweet Apple. Everybody else within hollering distance was an old settler, many of whom lived very much the way their parents and grandparents had lived when they came over the mountains in mule wagons. I looked around the chapel and found I was in company with a few survivors of that time — Miss Artie's relatives, some old neighbors and many gray-haired, slow-moving old friends whose ages approach her own eighty-eight years.

Were they remembering, I wondered, the pink-cheeked, bright-eyed, eighteen-year-old girl who came from Texas back when the century was young to marry Denver Cox, the son of Sweet Apple farmers, and settle down to rear her own family on that beautiful wooded land with its sweetly meandering little streams and a stillness broken only by bird calls and wind on the pine slopes? Were they remembering that when Miss Artie grew older, her mother-in-law died, and she and Denver and their three children moved into the old homeplace to look after her father-in-law? Were they remembering, as I was, her pleasure in her milk cows, her wonderful buttermilk and butter, the comfort of sitting in the kitchen by a shiny black wood stove on a winter day, waiting out a cake she had in the oven for company?

The old Cox homestead is no longer there. Denver Cox died and shortly afterward all the neighbors were invited to come to an auction that would dispose of most of the house furnishings and farming equipment. I cherish a crude little bench, homemade and stained with buttermilk and bluing, which Miss Artie told me was her "water bucket bench." In the days before electricity and pumps in wells, her water buckets were filled and sat on that bench just inside her kitchen door.

Miss Artie herself moved to a small, pretty apartment in Roswell. She missed the farm and her time there, but she rejoiced in conveniences and the comfort of central heat and milk and butter that came to her kitchen the easy way — no slogging through the muddy barnyard in winter rains to milk, no fighting heat and flies and worrying about snakes in the summertime, no straining and scalding and bottling of milk.

When she lived at Sweet Apple and we walked over to get milk and butter from her in early spring, we almost always went home with a bouquet of what Miss Artie called "johnny quills," the daffodils her parents-in-law planted sixty or seventy years ago. They were the earliest in the community and had that elusive fragrance only the old varieties seem to have.

When the house burned and brambles and underbrush took the yard, the johnny quills continued to come back faithfully every spring. I watched for them and usually hurried by to pick a few to take to Miss Artie in her town dwelling. If she was at home, we got in a visit, pure fun for me because she was a laughing, humorous, sweet-tempered woman with good memories of her early days in Georgia.

Among the passages of Scripture the minister at Miss Artie's funeral quoted was Proverbs' definition of a virtuous woman who "looketh well to ways of her household and eateth not the bread of idleness." Several of us found ourselves nodding solemnly in agreement with words well-chosen.

With Miss Artie gone, that stretch of Cox road is immeasurably saddened. I will think of her, but come April, I may not be able to pick her daffodils again.

January 15, 1989

*I*t's perfectly all right with me if Nancy Reagan wants to dictate decisions of state by consulting the stars or chicken entrails or whatever. At least she's doing it in the privacy of the White House, and, presumably, there are people such as Howard Baker on hand who can dilute or redirect her advice to the president. But I say keep her at home where the rest of the world won't view her pettishness and her bad manners.

Her behavior in the Soviet Union is an embarrassment to all American women who were reared to "act nice" when they go a-visiting. Admitting that Mrs. Gorbachev might not have been the easiest and most graceful hostess in the world — and I guess that's not surprising in a Russian — was that any reason for our president's wife to engage in a cat fight? When asked how she liked her hostess, did she need to lift her eyebrows, pause coyly and say, "We-ell, everybody's different"?

Diplomats and all American women I know would have been ready for that question. If their consciences wouldn't let them lie to the point of saying they liked the lady, they would have thought of something tactful or at least ambiguous to say.

"She's very charming," might have been more than Mrs. Reagan could stomach. How about "hospitable"? How about, "I'm so glad to have this opportunity to get acquainted with her"? That's indirection, of course, but reporters expect that of politicians, particularly when they want to evade the question or don't feel it's the right occasion to be forthright and honest.

And, of course, there's that old trick of answering a question with a question.

She might have said, "Hasn't she the loveliest coloring you ever saw? All this Russian cold brings out the roses in women's cheeks."

Instead of doing what any of the women back home would have done, there was Miss Nancy yapping, "I want to say something! I want to say something! OK?" I never did find out what she said when she managed to interrupt Mrs. Gorbachev. And suppose she didn't get a chance to say anything? She could count on innings with American reporters when she got home. In fact, she is probably already at work on a piece titled, "My Horrible Trip to Russia and How I Made a Fool of My Hostess."

When the Gorbachevs came to the United States, Mrs. Reagan was hardly more courteous. One of the moving scenes in William Campbell's novel "Big Beverage," an account of the early years of the Coca-Cola Company, was the scene where the company's top executive and his wife invited the new bottler in town to dinner. It was to have been just family and very informal, but the host looked out the window and saw the bottler and his wife puffing up the driveway decked out in dinner clothes. The sensitive executive and his wife rushed out of their street clothes into evening finery, determined not to make their guests uncomfortable.

Several people wrote to me about the Reagans' opposite handling of that situation when they had the Gorbachevs to dinner. They well knew that, right or wrong, the Soviets had some kind of set against dinner clothes and were bent on wearing street clothes. Wouldn't it have been consummately attractive if the Reagans had followed suit? After all, they don't have to prove to the American public that they *have* nice clothes and get gussied up for parties.

The only thing that cheers me about Nancy Reagan's behavior in the Soviet Union is that now we all know she's not material for the diplomatic corps. There's not a chance even George Bush, if he makes it to the presidency, will send her to Liechtenstein as our ambassador. Better we should have had Ethel Merman.

June 8, 1988

A Sibley Miscellany

From the Kitchen

*M*y youngest granddaughter Susy bragged to me recently that she can now cook waffles. "Can you, honey?" I said proudly. "Tell me how." "It's easy, Tine," Susy assured me. "All you have to do is put them in the toaster."

Well, I have had my share of Eggo and Aunt Jemima out of the frozen-food case, and they're not bad. They are handy to have in the freezer when sleepy young'uns come stumbling into the kitchen late on Saturday morning and normal, from-scratch breakfast is long since over. They even taste tolerable, if you warm your sorghum or south Georgia cane syrup and drown them in it.

But if you were raised on waffles as a sort of ceremonial meal, somehow it goes against the grain to have something as easy and unexciting as a freezer package and a toaster take over.

I remember when we discovered waffles in my childhood in Creola, Alabama (out from, that is). We had a wood range in the kitchen, a wonderful big green and yellow stove it was, which warmed us and fed us all winter and sometimes during the chilly rainy days of summer when the electric stove seemed a poor lackluster thing. There may have been electric waffle irons then, but we didn't know about them. My mother brought home a black iron one, built to be accommodated by one of the eyes on the woodstove.

It was, we all agreed, a wondrous device and we stood around respectfully and watched while Muv persuaded the fire in the stove to burn down to rosy coals and put the iron on to heat. Meanwhile, she brought out the big blue mixing bowl, the eggs and the milk, the sugar and the flour. The directions for this new venture into cookery were contained in a brand new book, which she must have acquired with the iron. It showed a gorgeous stack of this new delicacy with its elegantly arranged grids, its rich tawny color.

A lot of measuring and beating went on while the syrup heated in its pitcher set in a pan of water and the butter warmed in the warming closet. Even the plates were brought from the dining table and set at the edge of the stove to lose their winter chill. The thick golden batter was lightened by the addition of egg whites whipped to a foamy froth at the last minute and I can hear and smell it now as it was spooned into the hot iron.

All kinds of good things went with the waffles — streak o' lean fried crisp, country ham, sometimes chicken. But it's the waffle itself which I remember best. Nobody got a whole one, of course. They were divided into four sections and you started from behind, knowing the wondrous iron would never quite catch up with you. It did, of course. Before you ran out of waffle you always ran out of a place to put it and leaned back, warm and sticky and full-bellied.

We may have had waffles for breakfast. I remember them best for supper on a cold night. My mother's recipe book fell apart and some of it disappeared, but until her death I remember seeing the waffle recipe, butter and flour stained, in her kitchen cupboard. It wasn't there the last time I looked and that may be one explanation for what happened the other night. In a mood of remembering, I decided to go and buy a waffle iron. Not the kind I remembered, of course, but a shiny electric number. And then I couldn't wait to get it home and try it out. Waffles for supper, I announced, setting out the butter and eggs and reaching for the sifter.

The recipe I used was all right. The shiny iron performed efficiently. The south Georgia cane syrup was fine. We ate two apiece and I had to be the one to say it: Waffles don't taste like they used to.

December 2, 1980

*F*ashions in food are no more capricious than fashions in other things, I suppose, but has it ever occurred to you that many good things are lost and forgotten because they went out of style? Take fried steak, for instance. When have you heard of plain old-fashioned fried steak? I don't mean what they call country-fried, which turns up on menus in small town restaurants and boarding houses sometimes, all swimming in greasy gravy and simmered out of recognition. I mean crisp, brown, succulent *fried* steak.

Broiled steaks may have been around when I was a child. Somebody somewhere may have had a charcoal grill. Somebody may have known about garlic and butter being the natural accompaniments for steak, may even have called for steak inches-thick and rare. But I was full grown before I ever heard of such things. Come to think about it, hamburgers weren't the national food then either. We had ground beef, I suppose, but I don't remember that it was cooked in patties and served in buns. When we went to circuses and fairs and places where now fast foods are ubiquitous, we looked for hot dogs. Only we called them Coney Islands then.

🍎 🍎 🍎

But now fried steak, that was a weekly staple. It was, come to think about it, one of the first things I learned to cook. On a summer afternoon when my mother was busy in the yard she would often send me in to start supper. If there were no leftovers, which were the backbone of all suppers, and we weren't going to have something cold, it was fried steak. I can see her hands now, demonstrating the size of the lump of lard to be heated in the iron skillet. I can remember the precise directions for finding and using a certain heavy, yellowed crockery saucer, which was essential to "tenderizing" the steak. It was, of course, round steak and it was expected to be tough. Until you got through beating it with the edge of that old saucer, that is.

But if you were diligent about whamming the meat with the saucer, beating in your salt and pepper and as much flour as you could persuade the steak to take, the result was lovely.

The other afternoon I thought of those old encounters with saucer, steak and wood stove when I stopped by the grocery store. My father always cheered when we had fried steak for supper. (I guess he thought anything beat rice and cold milk.) It happened that there was good round steak in the meat case in front of me and I decided to give it a try. It has been years since I have tried this dish. Since childhood, I imagine.

But it wasn't hard to get back into the swing. I even had a heavy saucer for crisscrossing the grain of the meat with blows.

About halfway through the production I chickened out. Floured and browned, the round steak would be tough, I decided. The only way to redeem it would be to cover it with onions and simmer it in dark brown gravy. Which is a retreat to country-fried, of course, but I took it. Except for one small rectangle left in the skillet. Fried, just fried. I lifted it out with a fork and took a bite.

Now your fine fancy broiled sirloin is all right with me. Get it if you can and enjoy, enjoy. But I'm here to tell you that old tough fried round steak was simply wonderful. The salt and pepper and flour made a crunchy brown crust with a nut-like flavor. The meat itself was moist and tender and chewy with a beefy taste unlike anything you've experienced lately. Unless, that is, you're back to fried steak.

Of course, my family doesn't know about it. They got that stuff with the onions and gravy.

February 18, 1983

A friend of mine used to say she couldn't bear to eat lunch at a dime store lunch counter because her appetite was impaired by the sight of racks and bins of rayon bloomers. Well, rayon bloomers are no more and dime store lunch counters are scarce. But we have one in our neighborhood, and two youngsters, who presumably care only for McDonald's and Wendy's, put me on to Woolworth's turnip greens.

One day they asked me to dine there with them, and I'm here to report that they're on to something. I've been going back since, and I've never tasted better turnip greens—not even at my mother's table, and she was a peerless cook of all greens. She washed and picked them like Midas fingering crown jewels, removing any potentially bitter stems, immersing them in tepid water heavily salted to be sure no bugs were left on them and then washing them four more times. They were slowly and lovingly simmered and seasoned and came to the table chopped and crowned with bits of streak o' lean. Naturally, the essential accompaniment was corn bread and, if you could get it, home-churned buttermilk.

Near the first of the month, when Social Security checks make them affluent, you will see a lot of elderly women at this counter. There's one flamboyant old girl who wears picture hats atop a headful of orange curls, fluttering scarves of rich and splendid colors, chains and bangles and rings and ankle strap shoes. It is obviously her day on the town, and she lives it up, having the fried chicken and sweet potato pie, as well as a full complement of turnip greens and other vegetables.

We chat, if I happen to catch her, but she is rather grand and haughty and I really have a better time with the regulars, downtown workers, nurses aides and an occasional maid and a number of black men. I usually catch them when I am on the way to the MARTA station, and by now they know I'm going to be in a hurry.

"Turnip greens today?" I ask sociably.

"Collards," says a gruff-voiced domestic worker next to me.

"Good?" I inquire.

"Pretty good," she says grudgingly. "I put a spoonful of sugar in mine."

"They need it," says my neighbor on the other side. "You get 'em before frost sweetens 'em, they needs the sugar."

The waitress is busy and distracted, but my neighbors don't want me to miss either the collards or my MARTA train.

"She be's in a hurry," my left-hand neighbor tells her. "Collards 'bout all she gon' eat," says my right-hand neighbor.

"Ain't no corn bread today," I begin dolefully, "what have you got?"

"Ain't got hardly nothing," she says, chortling.

❦ ❦ ❦

Up and down the counter they take up the subject, turning it this way and that. Corn bread is essential and so is fatback. A person who tries to make do with ham hocks for seasoning is a poor, misguided cook and we all nod our heads in agreement. Fatback you've got to have.

These women, like me, were mama-raised greens cooks and their mama's rules, like mine, were fixed and immutable. You start with tender greens — not too much water, just enough for potlikker.

My little bowl of greens comes and, watching the clock, I tackle them fast.

"I got some broke-up corn bread," the waitress offers tentatively.

"I'll take it," I say eagerly.

"Me, too," echo my neighbors. "Broke-up don't hurt."

My greens are gone by the time the corn bread is delivered, but my left-hand neighbor points out that I still have a small emerald pool of potlikker in the bottom of the bowl. "Crumble and sop," she directs, and of course I do.

We part with goodbyes all around, and I rush for the MARTA train, strengthened and refreshed. My outing cost me sixty-five cents, not counting tip.

August 31, 1984

*O*f course, it's the weather that makes you gain weight. This is a theory brand new and original with me. I haven't encountered it in any weight-loss, how-to-be-skinny-and-gorgeous book yet, and even my fat friends who grasp at any excuse, haven't come up with that one.

It's my own, and I can prove that it's true. I made doughnuts the other day!

Now everybody knows that you don't go around making doughnuts on balmy days. With the kitchen windows open to bird song, bees and blossoms and sunshine, have you ever seen a doughnut simmering in hot grease? Of course not.

Absolutely the only time a woman will get out the flour and eggs and heat up a kettle of fat is on a chilly, windy, gray day when the temperatures plummet and you have a fire in the fireplace. Then, if ever, you start thinking of good rich, greasy, sweet food.

🍎 🍎 🍎

The funny thing about doughnuts is that I don't particularly crave them. Even at Dunkin' Donuts I might have a blueberry muffin with my coffee. I certainly never craved them enough to make them.

But the other night, waiting for a friend to take me to dinner, I wandered into a hardware store. There on a rack of kitchen appliances, shiny and tempting to all beholders, was a doughnut cutter. Now, I have never had a doughnut cutter. Biscuit cutters, yes. Pizza cutters, of course. But never a doughnut cutter — until that frosty evening. For $1.29, I bought my first one.

The next day was the first wintry-looking one of the season, probably not as cold as I thought it was going to be, but cold enough to warrant a hearth fire and something fragrant cooking in the kitchen. A pot roast in the old iron Dutch oven smelled fine enough, but it didn't smell particularly cold weatherish. So I got out the deep fat fryer a friend gave me and filled it with cooking oil.

🍎 🍎 🍎

That done, I looked around for recipes. Not surprisingly, there's a dearth of doughnut recipes in the newer cookbooks. The emphasis is on skinny food. I wouldn't even let myself crack one that emphasizes vegetables. I looked for the old "Settlement House Cookbook," reliable authority on sustaining victuals — thick soups and dumplings and goodies like that. Before I could remember where I had put that book, my hand fell on the "Uncommon Cookbook," out of New England. Now those women in that cold climate are probably the world's premier doughnut makers. Snowed in, as they must be off and on in the winter, they're certain to be suckers for fattening foods. Sure enough, there was a recipe for doughnuts, right next to several for fritters and cinnamon rolls.

The rain was falling, satisfactorily gray and cold-looking. Leaves shuffled around on the steps like a ghostly tramp begging for something to eat. And I fell to with rolling pin and doughnut cutter.

It wasn't a particularly complicated recipe. Somewhere I have one that calls for yeast. This one needed only flour, salt, sugar, cinnamon, nutmeg, sour milk, soda, baking powder and one egg. The mixture was a bit sticky, but it smelled good when it hit the hot fat and started sizzling.

And when I lifted the brown circles out of the cooker, they were crusty and gorgeous. Rolling them in granulated sugar was the final irresistible touch.

Of course, I didn't need to eat them. I know that. But with a fresh cup of coffee and that fire in the fireplace, I was doomed. I ate several. And now I know why they used to call them "sinkers." My diet program is sunk.

November 25, 1986

Women & Men

*A*s a woman's rightser I've just had my Road to Damascus. I have just seen the light.

Heretofore I have been concerned about equal pay and equal opportunity for women and less interested in whether our marital status was disclosed in the title before our names — Miss, Mrs. or a non-committal, unrevealing Ms. I have not felt abused or put down about dishwashing or bed-making, and it never occurred to me to doubt that sitting up with a sick child or sleeping on a cot by a bed in the hospital was woman's portion.

But why have women been saddled with housework all these years? Why, oh, why are women the ones who either move the dust around or feel guilty about it? The males of the world — with few exceptions, I'd better interpose before somebody accuses me of dealing in extravagant generalities — are the ones who leave greasy wrenches where they use them, dirty clothes where they step out of them, damp towels where they fall.

And if this disorder should be there when they come home from a wearisome day at work or school, you know who is a slob, a shirker, that worst of all things, a sloppy housekeeper.

All this struck me last week when I labored desperately to wash sheets, air pillows, neaten up the medicine cabinet, scrub the tub and mop the kitchen against the approach of some out-of-towners.

My mother, I realized, had made me believe this is woman's work and I am duty-bound to do it. She had a fairly valid point in her day. Her husband supported her, and she thought the least she could do was to have that impeccably "done up" shirt ready to his hands, socks carefully washed by hand and rolled together flawlessly matched. She also had a laundress and help in the kitchen from time to time.

Well, I haven't been supported by a man since my father did it many, many years ago. I went to work, and when I couldn't hire a cleaning woman — who can nowadays — I assumed that it was my responsibility to do the cleaning.

Suddenly it struck me the other day that mopping under the bed is boring, washing and mating socks is tedious and time-consuming and cleaning out the refrigerator a job so onerous no one person in a family should be saddled with it. It should be a share-and-share-alike project like eating the food which goes in and comes out of the refrigerator.

For the first time in my life I looked at the dirty jeans and old athletic socks which my grandson left on the floor by his bed as an insult to me. It's my fault that I have not required him to make up his bed and pick up his clothes when he's at my house, and the result is that he thinks he has more important things to do but that I haven't.

I don't mind working for the money to pay for groceries and going to the store and getting them, hauling them home and cooking and serving them. There's something relatively creative about that.

But I have finally come to realize that nobody in this world should expect somebody else to pick up his dirty clothes and wash them and dry them and sort them and put them away. It's belittling and demeaning, and I've had it.

April 25, 1980

*I*n this newspaper a couple of weeks ago we had a story about the trama of divorce for persons more than sixty years old. The loneliness, the feeling of displacement and rejection, the blow to the confidence were all delineated in poignant detail. But most devastating of all to many of the women involved was the financial blow.

Retirement and insurance go with the husband into his new marriage. So do most of the Social Security benefits. "If the former husband remarries," wrote Barbara S. Cain, of the University of Michigan, "his wife of a few years can, on his death, lay claim to an inheritance his wife of four decades cannot."

A friend of mine, who labors diligently for ERA and other feminist causes, must have been tempted to say, "I told you so!" when she read that. She has been telling anybody who would listen that for years. However, I heard from her shortly after that story appeared and, far from any evidence of triumph, she related a sad, first person experience in the same department.

A woman in her family, heretofore a tight-lipped and disapproving foe of ERA, has lost her husband to a younger woman — and with him went health insurance, life insurance, pension plan. Tortured by her own sense of failure, she is now job-hunting and fighting nightmares of "becoming a bag lady in her old age."

My friend shares her bitterness, although until this happened they had almost nothing in common. "Phyllis Schlafly and Marabelle Morgan are her heroines. I have heard her say, 'We don't need the ERA because God has given us the perfect plan for marriage. As long as the wife allows the husband to be in authority in all things, God will honor the marriage and preserve it.'"

My friend was more tolerant of that presumptuous statement than I might have been. (I'm always dubious of those who seem so privy to God's plan for them.) Calling it "a barnyard pecking order view of marriage and a perversion of Biblical teaching, which requires men, and not just women, to submit themselves to the needs of their mates," my friend said her relative bestowed on her "the scorn reserved for fools and heretics."

In spite of her tunnel vision she was apparently an excellent woman, in the Biblical sense, looking to the ways of her household with a vengeance. She worked hard to get her husband through law school and, once he was graduated, gave up a good job she loved "because he needed her at home" to "entertain the numerous political contacts important to his work as a lawyer and political lobbyist."

Being country-bred and no sissy, she entertained literally hundreds of people, including hordes of his relatives for an annual three-day family reunion.

"She idolized her husband and trusted him completely. When, a year ago, he startled her by insisting she enroll in law school, she was unenthusiastic but, thinking he wanted her to share more of his life, she studied hard and won acceptance into the law school of a local university.

"Now she figures his real intention . . . was to make himself look good in divorce court. ('She put me though law school, judge, so in fairness, she is getting the same opportunity she gave me.') Or maybe he just wanted her out of the way. While she attended night classes, he was free to pursue romance with the young divorcee he now plans to marry."

The wife's valedictory is familiar to us all. "What did I do wrong? I dieted until I was as thin as I was miserable and did everything else I could to be a perfect wife!"

But there's one more, eminently more practical quote from her, which makes the whole pitiful story worth reporting: "Married women are going to have to start using the strength of their vote to get some laws passed for their own protection!"

January 23, 1983

*W*hen we met in jail one Saturday night many years ago, my friend Margaret held some kind of record for multiple arrests. She was spending the night on a drunk charge. I was there to write a story about what Saturday night is like in the City Jail. She had sobered up by the time we met, and she was very gracious and hospitable to me, introducing me around to the jail regulars and inviting me to share the fish supper some of her relatives brought up to her before the evening was over. She wasn't proud of having been arrested one hundred seventy-five times or whatever it was, but when I asked her about it, she didn't flinch or evade the question.

"Lord, have mercy," she murmured. "Them's the breaks. And I don't know what it was for most of the time."

I knew. The police didn't leave me unenlightened long. She was a very busy, hard-working prostitute. They liked her and might have tried to avoid arresting her when they found her strutting past the Piedmont and Ansley hotels, all three hundred pounds of her. But she apparently had to get a little drunk before she could practice her profession, and when she got drunk she got loud and sometimes was found blocking traffic on Forsyth Street.

❦ ❦ ❦

So they hauled her into the police station and built up that arrest file. Margaret is old now and retired. I had trouble tracking her down, but I felt that it was urgent. A friend sent me a story about a sort of prostitutes' protective organization operating in San Francisco. I needed to know if the local sisterhood would approve it. It's called the U.S. Prostitutes Collective, and it was organized by a group of citizens who hope ultimately to abolish laws against prostitution.

Margaret Prescod, the San Francisco woman who was quoted by *The New York Times,* believes that prostitution is linked to poverty "as a cycle of absolute despair," that most women engaged in what she calls the "sex industry" are not criminals but victims and that penalizing them is immoral.

My friend Margaret sighed when I read her parts of the long *Times* story.

❦ ❦ ❦

"I don't half know what you're talking about," she said, "but the girls need help. I wouldn't a went into the business except my folks needed the money. My parents was old and sick, and I had a sister at home with a little bitty baby and no husband. She was married to a no-good-nik and finally took to hooking herself to help out. Lorda mercy, she hated it! She wasn't stout like me. I never seen no man I couldn't whup. But she come home many a morning all bruised and cut and messed up. Finally killed herself."

The notion that women go into the business for pleasure has been disproved again and again. But *The Times* did interview one young woman, who asked to be called Jane, who contended that it wasn't totally uncongenial employment.

"I enjoy my job," she said. "If I were a secretary I'd probably be complaining and organizing for better working conditions."

Looking back, I can't remember that any of the prostitutes I have known ever discussed that aspect of their job. I remember well going to what my mother called a "house of ill repute" with a classmate when we were both about fourteen and bent on playing hooky from high school. We knew it as her aunt's house, and we certainly didn't know that her aunt was a madam or that the pleasant, attractive young women we met there were prostitutes. They let us read their movie magazines and showed us how to "arch" our eyebrows and, after they had conferred with a couple of gentlemen callers in another room, they came in and ordered barbecue for the entire household, truant schoolgirls included.

I had no way of knowing of the hardships of their jobs, but it was plain that they weren't well-paid. They couldn't afford barbecue until very late in the day. I wish the U.S. Prostitutes Collective well.

April 9, 1984

A man I don't know called to ask me to play Dear Abby for him. He is miserably guilty and unhappy, he said, and thought that from my bountiful cache of tolerance and wisdom, I might cheer him up. What he really wanted, it developed, was for me to tell him he was not guilty of any wrongdoing and that everything is going to be peachy-dandy. (Isn't that what we all want?)

"I don't mind telling you," he said, "that I have been unfaithful to my wife."

"Ah," I murmured, "a lot of that is going around."

"Do you think that's so bad?" he said. "She has tried to kill herself. Isn't that pretty extreme?"

"Maybe she feels extremely bad about it," I muttered.

"She just wants to get even with me," he said. "Her pride is hurt, and she wants to make me feel awful because this girl . . . well, she's a nice young woman, very upright and honest and all, and I'm seeing her."

🍂 🍂 🍂

"Look, I can't talk to you about this stuff," I said. "I guess I'm prejudiced, but I think you've got something to feel rotten about, and your upright, honest young woman sounds like somebody I wouldn't trust around the corner. Go talk to a marriage counselor or a priest or a lawyer. I'm no expert."

"Aw, gee," he said boyishly. "I didn't think you'd be uptight about this. After all, you've been around. Is it too much to ask you to talk to me a little?"

"I'm busy," I said.

He sighed windily. "I apologize for taking your time. But I'm feeling pretty depressed, and my mama says you are a nice woman and might help me."

🍂 🍂 🍂

It suddenly seemed the worst kind of imposition to me. He doesn't want help. He wants reassurance. He wants to do what suits him and have somebody his mama thinks well of assure him that it's perfectly grand. Or, at the very least, that everybody's doing it. I made my mistake to mention that infidelity is pretty prevalent these days.

"Ok," I said at last. "I'll tell you what I think, and you're not going to like it. I think you are doing a thoroughly reprehensible thing, hurting people who love and depend on you and cheating in its lowest form. To cheat in business is probably something you'd scorn, but cheating on your marriage vows strikes me as even worse. You're cheating a person who trusts and depends on you — one you swore to cherish and protect. Is that what you wanted to hear?"

"Not hardly," he said with a regrettable lapse of grammar. "You're overlooking the fact that I'm in love with this girl. We love each other. It's big . . . "

"If you say it's 'bigger than both of us' I'm going to hang up in your face," I threatened.

"It is," he said soberly. "It's the real thing."

"That's Coca-Cola," I said waspishly.

"Look, you're not very sympathetic," he said. "My mama thought you'd have an answer."

"I told you I wouldn't have," I said. "I've got to go."

All afternoon, I seethed over his effrontery. I didn't want to hear about his great passion for this honest, upright darling who would probably knife her own mother or father in the back if it suited her. The thought of her and this red hot love affair made me want to emulate Dorothy Parker's "Tonstant Weader" and "frow up." Illicit, extra-marital love is such a tired old cliche, such a tacky, trashy exercise. Anybody who thinks he is going through a unique experience is crazy. It could be that the men and women who are faithful to a trust, kind and caring about the people who depend on them, selfless in their devotion are the unique ones. I hope not. I like to think there are still plenty of them around.

July 21, 1986

Chainsaws & Bulldozers

*U*ntil this year the quiet of an April afternoon in the country was one of the loveliest things in the world. You could stand ankle-deep in the greening, surging grass and listen to a stillness so steady and unbroken you fancied you heard clouds moving, anemones opening, the soft whisper of water in the underground streams which fill the well.

If a mockingbird sounded it was an explosion. The passage of a jet miles away was a tumult. Every murmur was accentuated by the soundless air. But clamor has come to the country. Cars and motorcycles and trucks of all sizes and purposes roar by on our dirt road. Power saws whine through the afternoons.

Our late neighbor, Denver Cox, once gee-hawed his mule through rows of corn and bean fields and it made a kind of sweet and lonesome country music. The Johnson's banty rooster crowing for day was a happy chanson. We heard an occasional hound dog baying at the moon, whip-poor-wills at twilight and mourning doves at noon.

Now we hear machines and the pitiless crash of trees, making way for the new subdivisions. The woods which once encompassed us are thin now, as see-through as a summer dress without a petticoat. New and ominous signs are all about us. Sign boards giving notice of a rezoning hearing. Sign boards heralding a new subdivision with a cutsey-county name and a fresh cut split rail fence, not because it's the only kind of fencing available as in the old days in the mountains but because it is now country chic.

The day my neighbors' guineas discovered my yard and came potracking through I vow I thought they were stage props put out by real estate agents. I fully expected to see a goose girl driving a gander down the road, a mule and wagon and maybe a milk cow show up at any minute.

🍂 🍂 🍂

But those guineas at least are real and the noise they make, a raucous pandemonium, delights my ears as they delight my eyes. They are odd looking birds with their long-legged turtle shape but as sedate and impeccable in their gray and white as Quaker ladies at meeting. Watchdogs, my neighbor said, guaranteed to alert you to snakes and visitors. I don't know about snakes. They raised a ruckus in my plum thicket the other day. But I think the hubbub of land clearing, road-building, ditching and culvert setting, has made them immune to people.

If the impending rush of neighbors to the old fields and pastures and woods around us meant one-at-a-time settlers, as in the old days, I think we would all be more hospitably inclined. I remember hearing one of the old-timers down the road speak happily of the days when my house was a school house and there were enough people in the settlement for socials. There was comfort in seeing smoke from a chimney within hailing distance in those days of bad roads, slow transportation and no telephones.

So far we haven't met a neighbor we didn't like but then we haven't met them all, not by a long shot. So we measure the time we have left hour by hour. When it rains and the bulldozers are quiet we savor the tranquility. One more day we have of country stillness, one more night when the moon can shine unchallenged by street lights.

Nothing lasts forever and that knowledge sharpens and sweetens the now. I fill a tiny cream pitcher with violets and think one spring at the time, just one spring at the time . . . !

April 8, 1980

he property has been sold, the little house on the hill back of the cluster of community mailboxes is lonesome and deserted. The latest word is that the new owners will bring a bulldozer any day and push it down. I don't know what they're going to build there, but they will have a hard time making it as attractive to us old settlers as the little house that stood there.

By current building standards, I guess it wasn't much of a house — four rooms, made snug and warm by yellow fake brick siding; a privy and a hog pen and a chicken yard in the back; a chuckling, crackling wood heater in the front room, the smell of cornbread baking and white beans cooking from the litte kitchen.

The house was built by Clarence Johnson for his first wife Olivia; after her death, he made improvements and equipped it with indoor plumbing for his second wife, Mary Lee. And always it was a beacon of "nigh-neighbors" and helpfulness to the rest of us.

When we came in from town at night, it was cheering to see lights in that little house on the hill. When we got a car stuck in the mud, as we did rather frequently twenty years ago, we knew somebody with a tractor would come chugging down the hill to help us.

The first visitors we had at Sweet Apple were Clarence and Olivia, who brought a sack of sweet potatoes from their garden and a windlass for our well.

"We're proud to have you for neighbors," they said, as welcoming words as I ever heard.

They can build a million-dollar mansion on that hill, if they are of a mind to, but I doubt if the parties they give will be as much fun as the ones we've known there, when the Johnson family and their kinfolks picked up fiddle and banjo and guitar and opened up the old pump organ and cracked down on "Soldier's Joy," "Finger Ring," and "Soap Suds Agin the Fence." And I seriously doubt if the new owners will ever have the prime cold weather festival known as hog killing, when neighbors gather to turn fattened shoats into sausage, hams, cracklings and middlings.

By some standards, the people who lived in that little house weren't rich, but if wealth means having enough and being able to share, they were millionaires. Their summer gardens always yielded beans and corn and okra and tomatoes for their family and their neighbors. One year, I remember, they planted a surprising number of pumpkins. "You can only use so many pumpkins," I said when I saw the plenteous harvest.

"Ain't any trouble to grow 'em," Mrs. Johnson said, "And we like to have them to give."

The scrubby apple trees in their yard weren't picturebook lush, but they bore richly, and in later summer, one of the delights of the settlement was the apple-pepper relish that filled the kitchen with a sweet vinegary aroma.

When that house was built there weren't any million-dollar mansions around, and it seemed convenience enough to have a "good well of water," as Olivia's father, Mr. Lum Crow, put it.

They not only had a good well of water but it was so close to the house that, in time, they were able to surround it with a good back porch, eventually enclosed to make a spacious, sunny room. They had a sink in the kitchen, which was modern convenience enough for the times, and a water barrel on the roof that supplied soft rainwater in season.

The day they come with a bulldozer to push that house down, I hope I am a thousand miles away. It's the last landmark left from the days when this part of north Fulton County was still country, except for the nice white house down the road that belonged to the Chamlee family. Jettie Bell Johnson, who was a Chamlee, smiled ruefully when she told me about the bulldozer's coming.

"Some day, I reckon they'll push this house down, too," she said.

I looked around the pretty kitchen with its mixture of modern conveniences and old family cupboards, and I felt like crying. But how long can any of us hold out against high-priced developments that are called progress? My old Sweet Apple log cabin, now nearly 150 year sold, has probably overstayed its time, too.

January 29, 1986

*T*he children said, "Don't go. Don't subject yourself to that!" But I *would* walk out the door and through the woods to see what the developers are up to. What they're up to is putting in wide streets with curbs and rearranging the earth to make way for a suburban neighborhood. My dog Kazan and I were ankle-deep in red clay most of the time, but we got a good look at it, and I'm sure it's going to be perfectly splendid.

People have to live somewhere, and real estate people have to make a living and growth is inevitable. Or so I keep telling myself. And to give it authority, I said some of it aloud to Kazan.

"Here's where the Sweet Apple dogs used to cut through the woods to the lake," I told him. "When we'd get in the truck, they seemed to know we were heading for the lake, and they tore through the woods to beat us there. Lady was the fastest of all . . . ."

But Kazan exhibited his own speed by getting out of hearing. And I was left to slog along behind him, remembering. On that bank over there, according to neighborhood lore, they used to post one of our good friends with his shotgun to look out for the revenuers. When the officers showed up, he was to fire a shot to warn his friends and relations down by the creek so they could make a quick getaway.

🍎 🍎 🍎

But he was a very sedentary type, my late friend and neighbor, and if he sat still long enough, he inevitably went to sleep. The night they had him posted as a lookout, he was so sound asleep the revenuers took his shotgun and his hound dog and went on with the raid.

With a new house and possibly a paved parking area or a swimming pool there, who will remember? The muscadine vines that our friend Quinton showed us are no longer there. In fact, I couldn't find the tree where they hung in blue-black swags. Or the little pink wild roses that grew on that bank are gone. The maidenhair ferns that grew on that bank are gone. The clearing where I picked up light'ard knots is no clearing now but has a big brick house on it.

Trees have been uprooted and great massive stumps scattered along the roadside, making it difficult to wander off to see if the view of old Sweat Mountain is still good from that point, or if the rhododendrons and wild azaleas that bloomed there are doing all right. We walked that road often when we first moved to the country, and sometimes on weekends, we had picnics beside it, after we had helped to clear it of brush or followed along behind a borrowed road patrol, which was expected to make it passable.

It did help, but not until everybody in the family had been stuck on the road at least once. I have a mental picture of my daughter with one baby in arms, and another one on the way, tramping up the muddy hill in the rain to report that her little car was immobilized by "red gook."

The lake was the thing that drew us. All of us helped to build it, lugging brush to be burned, seeding the dam with grass, setting out little pines to hold the eroding clay bank. All the children learned to swim there, and the bigger ones helped to haul sand and spread it to make a beach for the babies who could not venture into the deep water. We fished there and watered their Christmas gift donkeys, Jack and Jenny, and many times, we picnicked there.

Like all bodies of water, it drew life. Birds dipped down there at twilight. Frogs filled the evenings with their cacophony. Fish darted, water bugs skimmed the surface and late one evening, as we sat beside it, we watched a snake move across it.

The lake has been drained, my grandson told me. The lake is no more. I dreaded to see, but Kazan was off in the underbrush somewhere so I plodded doggedly on, determined to see the worst. To my astonishment, there was water in the lake — not much, to be sure, far from enough to fill it. But there in the middle of the dark water was Kazan, happily swimming! For some reason, I felt immeasurably cheered.

September 3, 1986

*T*he note from our rural mail carrier instructed us to move our mailbox from the crossroads to our house — and, of course, we'll do it with all possible speed.

I wouldn't dream of defying the U.S. government, especially that branch having to do with the mails. (I assume Uncle Sam still has his fingers on the mails, even if there is some kind of contract arrangement now.) But even as we look for a new mailbox and a post to tack it on and post-hole diggers to plant it in the earth, I hope the post office knows it is breaking my heart.

Anybody can have a mailbox in front of his home. Suburbanites and lots of city people get their mail that way. But a cluster of mailboxes up at the crossroads is pure country.

It is the way country people have always received their mail — not from a box attached to their front door, not from a box down at the foot of their driveway beside a street, but from a battered old tin receptacle sociably set up at the crossing, with the mailboxes of the nearest neighbors.

The morning walks to the crossroads were part of the ritual. No dashing out in housecoat and slippers, but what a neighbor of mine called "wearing clothes," because we were going to be seen when the mail, as we said, "run."

🌱 🌱 🌱

There would be a convocation of women and children waiting for the carrier — to buy stamps, collect a package from Sears, Roebuck and Company or maybe a long-awaited letter from a son or daughter. It was a season of sociability.

Now there are a lot more people in our settlement; too many, I realize, for a homely row of dented and rusting old boxes beside the paved road. Each fine new house has its own mailbox now, sometimes cunningly hidden in a rock structure of some kind, sometimes leaning toward the mail carrier's reach with garlands of clematis or roses growing over and around it.

Our new neighbors are very tasteful with their mailboxes. You don't see any wooden Uncle Sams in striped pants and starry jackets extending mail receptacles. It's been years since I saw Future Farmers and Future Homemakers concrete box holders. Sometimes you run into an old plow that has been pressed into service to give a mailbox a kind of old-time rural panache. But I haven't seen a heavy chain all welded together to hold it in a firm "S" shape eternally or a wagon wheel in a good while.

❦ ❦ ❦

Except for hiding them in rock strongboxes, either to match a nearby wall or to keep young delinquents from shooting holes in them or banging into them in their parents' pickup trucks, new home builders in our area are being frank and open and uncoy with their mailboxes. That's all to the good, but it is not crossroads mail service, and I'm going to miss that.

When we moved to the country, the first thing we did after unloading the furniture was to go up to Chadwick's store and buy a mailbox. My son got some black paint to keep it from rusting and some white paint for lettering on our name; and, when it was in place, we drove by it three or four times, feeling a great sense of at-homeness. We liked keeping track of our neighbors by whether they had received a package too big for the box or put up the little red flag because they were dispatching something. When a box became choked with newspapers, we speculated that the owners were visiting their kinfolks in North Georgia.

Now the boxes are disappearing as, one by one, the old crowd of settlers is told to move them. The neighbors are dispersing, and getting and sending mail ain't what it used to be.

July 29, 1987

Of Clothes & Cars

*N*obody has ever said I had an excessive love of clothes. In fact, a more clothes-conscious friend of mind really applied these classic put-downs to me: "Do you like that as well as what they're wearing this year?" and "My, you certainly have gotten a lot of wear out of that!"

It's been my lifetime failure to only think about clothes when I absolutely have to have them. Even my mother, who was a far dressier type, deplored the way I once ran by a store on the way to the airport and bought a winter coat. She agreed that I needed it in Richmond, my destination, but she thought it was a cavalier way to choose a garment from which I hoped to get years of service.

My mind usually wanders when clothes is the subject. Except, and this is a little depressing, I usually love my old clothes with a strange sentimental attachment a saner woman would reserve for a puppy or a kitten or even a favorite kitchen utensil.

I admire my friend Pokey who makes a practice of turning out her closet once a year, and if she hasn't worn a garment in the past twelve months, she finds somebody to give it to. (Usually me, thank goodness.)

It is not only generous but sensible. Why keep an old coat you never plan to wear? Why crowd your already too-small space with stuff you'll never put on your back again? And yet . . .

Well, there was a day when I valiantly tried this approach. Whole and useful garments that I knew I was through with I passed on to my daughters. Moth-eaten and hopelessly dated garments went in a stack to be hauled to the county landfill at Morgan Falls. I had saved some of them for five or ten years in the wistful hope that I would one day make a splendid all-wool braided rug. But the day I had my closet cleaning, I knew I'd never have time for that.

It wasn't easy, the decisions. That good blue suit that was first mine and then my mothers . . . ah, it should be saved for something! The red polyester dress I always hated brought me no qualms, but the gray skirt, the good gray skirt . . . I turned it this way and that wondering if it was possible to mend it. If I could sew patches over the moth holes?

Finally, it went into the pile, and I squatted on the floor remembering the day my daughter, long since departed for New Jersey, took me to a wonderful junk store where they were selling lengths of fabric for pennies.

Here was gray wool, the kind used for men's suits, in sufficient quantity to make a skirt. Price fifty cents. I took it home, stitched it up and wore it with great pleasure, even buying some gray suede boots one winter to go with it.

The boots were given away years ago. The gray skirt went on and on — first to work and then to the grocery store and then on woodland trips. A splendid garment.

Hauling it out to the truck for the trip to the dump was traumatic. I averted my face and thought about higher things. Would Henry David Thoreau mourn a fifty-cent gray skirt? Would that philosopher who said, "Beware of enterprises requiring new clothes" have any patience with my attachment for a mere garment?

The truck loaded with castoffs from all over the house went on to Morgan Falls, and I forgot about my loss for two or three days. Then the other morning as I headed home from my walk I saw something by the roadside. Dew-wet and half-hidden by weeds was my good gray skirt! It had fallen off the garbage truck.

I picked it up and folded it tenderly and hid it under by T-shirt, in case some of my neighbors passed and saw that I had retrieved it.

It hangs in the closet again — not for keeps, just until I get up the strength to throw it away.

August 24, 1983

*M*y daughter had a little heart-to-heart talk with me. I should, she said, go buy myself some clothes and "fix up a little." I listened respectfully.

She is my New Jersey daughter, and she is the kind of person who emptied out a big bookshelf, put the books on the floor and filled the shelves with shoes. I had to speak to her about that. Nobody needs that many shoes, I told her, and it was sinful and extravagant and downright selfish to have more of anything than you need.

She pointed out that she had left to me Henry David Thoreau and his wise sayings about possessions. ("Simplify! Simplify! . . . Many of the luxuries, and many of the so-called comforts, of life are not only not indispensable, but positive hindrances to the elevation of mankind.")

It was her observation, she continued, that everybody is willing to eschew some things — like me and fur coats — and then we go all out on something else like me and my regular tryst with Strand's big bookstore. I can no more read all the books I lug home than she can wear all those shoes, she pointed out.

🍒 🍒 🍒

Besides, she said, grinning, she doesn't know about mankind in general, but having the exact pair of shoes she needs for an occasion is pretty elevating to her.

So we talked and I brooded on her counsel. Buy clothes, fix up. What I forgot to ask was, "Why?"

There must be good sense in all this shopping and primping. So many people are going it. I know a lady with a hundred lipsticks, for instance. And only one pair of lips. She says she buys clothes for the good of her morale, which has been at a very low ebb recently. I mentioned that either she had the most pampered morale in this vicinity or an extremely pragmatic one. Imagine a morale that would straighten up and fly right just because its owner bought a new pair of pink pants — with shoes to match.

My morale does not exactly soar into outer space, but it's not in such a state of disrepair either. When I feel low, it's usually about something a new frock with matching shoes wouldn't help at all. In fact, buying clothes is depressing. It points up too clearly that skipping ice cream the other night didn't trim off a single pound.

And then the cost! That $12.98 dress you used to find in your size has long since disappeared from the racks. The shoes I squandered $2.98 on are now $75. Only two years ago I essayed to be well-shod. I bought three pairs — the identical plain, medium-heeled pump I have always worn — in blue, brown and black.

❧ ❧ ❧

Who could ask for anything more? Only people who don't like scuffed heels and toes, of course. The shoe repairman's prices have gone out the roof, and you can't get a heel repaired while you wait for a dollar any more. It will cost almost as much as a pair of new shoes. So I wear 'em scuffed generally, and I have to count on the public to neither care nor notice.

Unfortunately, my sharp-eyed daughter did notice. Shop, paint your face, curl your hair, she said. And, woe is me, I forgot to ask why.

It would be different if I could walk into a fitting room and emerge like a butterfly from a chrysalis. In with the grub, out with the butterfly.

In my case, it's in with the grub and out with the grub all gussied up.

Now I know Elizabeth Taylor can be a revoltingly obese old girl with a gooked-up face one day and a blooming beauty who looks not a day older than twenty the next. But being beautiful is Miss Taylor's bag. Did I need to assure my daughter it is not mine? I doubt it.

She remembers too well the denim skirt I wore with a nail to hold it closed. She remembers that I didn't know what a young girl was talking about when she said she got a "body curl" in her hair.

She remembers the gentlemen who took me dancing, only to behold that I was wearing one blue shoe and one black shoe. She also knows, I'm afraid, that her advice fell on barren ground.

October 25, 1987

*P*eople should not sell their old and well-loved cars. There should be no more traffic in good and faithful vehicles than there is in good and faithful watchdogs. If a car has served you well, its sturdy gears meshing subtly with your feebler flesh-and-blood gears, you should put it out to pasture as you would a horse or an old aunt, when you no longer need it.

There are a lot of reasons for not selling your old car. The trauma of parting is something you take into account when you put that ad in the paper, having already embarked on a flirtation, or worse, with a younger, newer model. We had to have a truck in our family. All country people need trucks for hauling wood and garbage and the kids to the lake on a summer afternoon. So we found one — not new, but new enough to have some frivolous things like push-button windows and a noisy whine to warn and reproach if you leave the keys in the ignition or the lights on. All pearls before swine, as far as I'm concerned. Otherwise, I liked it and willingly drove it.

Then they told me, those cooler masculine heads in the family, that I better sell my little Pacer. It's expensive to have an extra car sitting around, needing insurance and shoes and stuff like that. So I let them advertise. There was no mad rush of eager customers, I noticed, but there was a little interest.

❧ ❧ ❧

And I hated every person who came to look. One critical prospect eyed my car like it was a blind and spavined old horse. They raised questions. Why did the hatchback lid do like that? Ha-ha, I said gaily, a mere crotchet, a little whim. Something happened to the thingamajig whch holds it up but I've been using my head when I load and unload groceries for a couple of years. Nothing to it.

That smell, that *unusual* smell in the interior? Nothing unusual about it. When baby bottles get spilled you can't really get up all the milk. Sometimes it takes years to get accustomed to the delicate fragrance of sour milk. I don't find it offensive. Those marks on the seats? Anybody knows a three-year-old with a crayon in his hand will leave marks on the seats. Personally, I find them attractive.

Then a pushy young man with a tactless streak in him lifted the hood. It was exactly like the time I took our ancient cousin to the doctor for her first physical — a humiliation, an invasion of privacy.

"I don't want to sell it," I said sulkily. "It's too good to sell."

❦ ❦ ❦

And it is, but there's yet another reason for keeping it: What my daughter calls "those little pieces of paper." You can't just let your faithful old friend go to alien hands and go back in the house and lick your wounds. You have to turn out dresser drawers, rifle the desk, dump the contents of pocketbooks on the kitchen table. All to find out that you don't have that little piece of paper which says you own your old car and have a right to sell it.

My daughter cried the last time she had to make a five-hour trip to the capital of New Jersey to get the title of a car. "Don't cry, honey," I pleaded. "It's nothing to cry about."

"Mother," she said darkly, "some people commit murder or suicide for less."

It's true. I know it's true, although I live closer to our capital and have found the people in the title department friendly and helpful. But if they punish me with a ten-day wait and demands for affidavits and birth certificates and Social Security numbers, I won't blame them. I shouldn't be selling my old car.

February 2, 1983

*T*here may be other horrendous things you can do to a man when he's down and out in a hospital room suffering a pretty grave illness. I think I did the worst: I wrecked his car.

Now my husband, Jack Strong, brought to our marriage an aging Lincoln Continental that had been in his family a couple of years before he got it. His cousin in Houston, after the manner of Texans, buys big cars. When he was ready to trade one in several years ago, he offered it to Jack, a proposition I wouldn't have been able to refuse, and I don't even like big shiny automobiles. Jack did like that one. He loved it. He kept it curried and groomed like a prize stallion. Once he had it repainted. Once he squandered a vast amount of money to replace a window vent. (I would have stuck a pillow in it.) He knew the folly of loving *things*, but he did love that car.

And the afternoon when he was feeling his worst, ready to turn his face to the wall in the hospital and, as we used to say in the country, picking at the cover, his mother and I, tired and disconsolate, got in the big Lincoln for the trip to Sweet Apple. Julia is a little woman, frail after several bouts with illness and dependent on a cane as, she says, "a third leg." But we talked cheerfully of other matters as we hit the cool country air and an almost traffic-free stretch of Highway 140.

Suddenly I saw a little car coming at us from a side road, and suddenly we were hit a smashing blow that turned us crosswise on the highway. The right front of Jack's pretty old car was a mangled mess, and his mother and I were gibbering idiots for a moment or two.

"You hurt?" we asked one another when we were able to speak.

Then I ran to check the driver of the other car—a woman who seemed dazed and flattened out on a seat that had apparently shaken loose from its moorings and fallen backward.

"Don't move her!" somebody behind me cried. "An ambulance is on the way!"

I ran back to let Julia out of her son's car and couldn't open the door.

"Never mind," she said and climbed nimbly out the left side under the steering wheel, pulling her cane behind her.

All accidents are bad, and that wasn't the worst one I ever saw, I suppose. The other driver apparently was hospital treated and sent home. Police and wreckers came, and one valiant couple of splendid character came forward and told me they had been driving toward us and witnessed the accident and here were their names and telephone number if we needed them. In the commotion that followed, I forgot for awhile that my passenger and I were stranded by the roadside with night coming on. All the official cars had errands elsewhere. Jack's car was, in the brutal words of the tow-truck man, "totaled."

It was all very bleak, but suddenly things began looking better. A couple who are friends of friends saw us standing there, pulled over and offered us a ride. We may be involved with insurance people for a time, but the next day Jack's Texas cousin arrived at his bedside and eventually, the bedside of the mortally wounded Lincoln.

"Don't worry," he said. "I have another one, same age (nine years), same size. I retired it a while back, and I'm going to get it to you."

It's a pretty car, even I have to admit, white instead of navy blue, and we are privileged to have the use of it in these upsetting days. But I worried about telling Jack and didn't really get around to it until the other day when they let him out of the hospital.

"Where's my car?" he asked reasonably, as he waited in a wheelchair at the hospital door.

"It was so worried over your illness," I said hastily as my grandson, John, came around the corner in it, "it turned white overnight!

September 2, 1988

Celebrations

A brand new year is a cheering, spirit-lifting prospect, I don't care how many good resolutions are foredoomed. We all know it's going to be fraught with problems and grief and pain, as all years are. Never imperishably glad, as it is put forth in Tennyson's poem about the May queen. ("Tomorrow will be the happiest time of all the glad New Year; Of all the glad New Year, mother, the maddest, merriest day.") But you have to admit that "new" has a very promising sound. Anything can happen. Anything can be.

Think of all the familiar sayings in which you encounter new: "A *new* nation, conceived in Liberty and dedicated to the proposition that all men are created equal." . . . "This nation, under God, shall have a *new* birth of freedom." "A *new* commandment I give unto you, that ye love one another." New birth. New society. New Deal. New Frontier. New world.

Of course, there are some bad connotations too, but better not to think of those as we face this unused, untried, umblemished swatch of time.

A funny thing to me has always been how people cling to New Year's superstitions. A smart young man, recently graduated from an impressive eastern college, came by the other day to ask me if I knew any New Year's superstitions. About the only ones I do remember, I told him, have to do with that day.

Reared in Atlanta, he believes, he confessed with a laugh, that black-eyed peas and hog jowl are absolutely essential to assure prosperity and well-being for the coming year.

"Have you never skipped them?" I asked.

"Never!" he said.

"And you've always flourished?"

He laughed. "There have been some bad years," he said, "but think how much worse they would have been if I'd missed my black-eyed peas."

I shuddered to contemplate the sinister possibilities. As far as I remember, we've never missed the New Year's standard, even during the Depression years of the 1930s. My mother faithfully scrubbed a dime and sterilized it and put it in a bowl of peas, convinced it would bring riches to the person who got it or to the house if left in the bowl. And I suppose, relatively speaking, we have been rich. At least, we have had food and shelter adequate to our needs — and how much richer would you want to be?

But not all New Year's superstitions are upbeat. When I was a child in the country, our neighbors firmly believed that anything you did on New Year's Day you would do all year.

❦ ❦ ❦

The trouble was that there were so many things you dared not do. If you picked up a bit of sewing and took a few stitches, you would "sew for a corpse before the year is out." If you swept a floor, dire things were due to happen — death or the arrival of evil enemies. A man who dared to pick up a hammer and nails or a saw was doomed to make a coffin during the next twelve-month — and so on.

"Don't kiss a boy on New Year's," an old woman warned us. "You'll be bound to marry him if you do. And you may not want to, you know."

It's important to tell your bees, if you have a hive, "Happy New Year" or they'll leave home and presumably leave disaster in their wake. Don't kill an ant on New Year's Day or his brothers and sisters will fall to and dig your grave. If you go fishing, don't step on your line. Terrible luck on New Year's Day. If you go hunting, stay clear of cemeteries. Ghosts come out and, who knows, you may waste your ammunition shooting at vapors.

So many ill omens, so many taboos could make us all nervous about the New Year, if there are any believers among us. I think they are interesting only in that they indicate how important, how momentous this day was to people in the past. May it be at least that much to all of us.

December 30, 1983

*I*t was getting on toward 11 A.M. and there were a lot of them lined up at the back door to St. Mark United Methodist Church. Mostly men, I noticed, and some of them had that too humble, eager-to-be-nice look of old winos. Some averted their faces in embarrassment as I went by, and I guess they saw I wasn't going to join their ranks and ask for a sandwich for lunch and they were embarrassed. One woman, seated on the steps, lifted an intelligent face and gave me a half-smile. She had spread out in her lap the paper she had been reading.

This scene is played out daily and nightly at many Atlanta churches. So many people have no food to eat, no bed and roof of their own. It makes the to-do over gourmet cooking and Easter finery seem not only silly but downright calloused.

How can anybody who has seen that humble, patient, embarrassed lineup of people waiting for bread or a bed go jubilantly into self-indulgence? It makes even the gala plastic baskets and the indigestible sugary eggs we put together for children seem excessive. Someone told me that as hard as they try, the volunteers in the church kitchens often don't have enough food to go around.

"If I could have one Easter wish," a church member in an apron told me, "it would be that I would never have to close the door in the face of the hungry or the homeless. Unfortunately, we haven't the divine gift of stretching our loaves and fishes to feed our multitude."

Even in that group of supplicants outside church doors, Easter, the holiest of church days, comes with a special meaning. Most of them will not be going into the sanctuaries on Easter morning to hear the choirs and the sermons and to say their prayers. They would be ashamed to in their soiled clothes. But they are no less glad of the day.

For to all of us, Easter is proof of miracles beyond human ken. We can be hungry and down on our luck. Jobs that we can do might seem non-existent, the world a mostly cold and unfriendly place except for that light kept burning in the churches. But Easter is a reminder that the world can be born anew, that life can change, that good things beyond our understanding do happen.

"I don't deserve what's happening to me," an old man told me, and I mistook his words for a complaint.

"I mean the good things," he said. "That tree. . . ." He pointed to a dogwood about to bloom. "The sunshine. . . . What have I ever done to deserve such beauty?"

He had a point. Few of us deserve the good things that happen to us. Or most of the bad things, although I was reared to believe that bad things were the results of my own sloth or folly. Easter Sunday is the miracle that is given to us undeserved, unearned. Even the pagans, not believing in Christian resurrection, recognized this spring day as a triumph over the death of winter, as proof of another chance at life, a new beginning.

May it be just that for all the weary tribe who wait outside churches.

They are Old Testament lines so are not said of Easter. But the Psalmist who said with the bread lines and the bed-beggers, "I am forgotten as a dead man . . . I am like a broken vessel," also said, "Weeping may endure for a night but joy cometh in the morning."

Easter proves it.

April 1, 1983

*T*he approach of Mother's Day started me thinking of her—a hardworking practical nurse who reared her children, ran a pretty, impeccably-clean house, never missed Mass at her parish church, never failed to offer food, furniture, money and love to anybody who needed it. I always thought she was a paragon of motherhood, and then, I inexplicably got enmeshed in a conversation with her daughter-in-law.

"She lies," said the daughter-in-law bluntly. "I think she's senile. Her house is dirty. She told me the sheets on her husband's bed were fresh—and they weren't. She almost ordered me out of the house when I checked and started changing the bed. She had pots soaking under the sink. The carpet. . . oh, you should have seen it!"

Her children did see it, and they went right to work—a self-appointed cleaning crew. They fired the day worker she loved because the woman was good company but no good as a cleaner. They hired a cleaning woman she hated on sight. They, her children, love her but they are driving her crazy.

Her house is no longer her own, but a place which they will inspect and criticize at any moment they want to. Her role as the wise and good mother whose food they ate happily, whose house was warm and welcoming, has been shattered.

❦ ❦ ❦

They don't understand what has happened to her, and she is beginning to worry about herself. They say she is forgetful and, of course, she is. But it makes her nervous to try to talk to them. They will catch her on some lapse. She lent them money to start their businesses, she gave comfort and help all the years they needed it. Now she can't reconcile herself to the needs they see in her.

Before I started calling the daughter-in-law and other members of that family cruel and insensitive, I perceived the mote in my own eye. During my mother's last illness, I washed every window in her house, cleared out cupboards she hadn't opened in years, hauled out paper bags she had apparently been saving since World War II.

"Come and sit on the porch and let's talk," she would invite.

But I didn't have the time. Now I realize how wrong I was.

The trouble is, that in the name of love, older parents are robbed of dignity and independence. We re-cast them in roles of dependence and senility. Anybody of any age might forget that old Mrs. So-and-So who used to live near us died fifteen years ago. But let a mother in her eighties forget it and she's senile. Many young housekeepers might be slow at changing the beds for a variety of good reasons. This mother was pegged as dirty and a liar because she let it slide and then tried to keep her daughter-in-law from finding out.

❦ ❦ ❦

While we're celebrating Mother's Day today, it's all very well to give her housecoats and nightgowns she probably doesn't need and will give away next Christmas. Candy and flowers will make a nice arrangement on the coffee table, but she doesn't eat sweets any more and she'll deplore your extravagance at buying florist flowers when she has those she really values blooming in the backyard.

What she wants from you is first, love — not sappy, greeting-card love which endows her with virtues she never claimed, but unswerving love which accepts her as she is and respects her in spite of her errors. She may be slower than she was when she sat up with you on croupy nights. She may not be able to reach in the old sock and share her savings with you anymore. She may not set a fine table these days. But she's a person, the same person really, and she doesn't want to be patronized or pampered like a pet cat. She wants to run her own life, maybe not as efficiently as you're running yours, but as well as she can for as long as she can. This advice I offer to abide by for Mother's Day. I'm sorry I didn't myself on Mother's Day 1976.

May 13, 1984

*T*he Depression was still on the land when my three-year-old cousin came to live with us. His father was ill with tuberculosis and his mother didn't know what to do with the child. My mother knew. She got in the car and drove straight away to the ramshackle homemade trailer in which they lived. It was on a Florida beach, near the father's last job, painting a big bridge.

Terry's mother cried to see him go. She had his few clothes packed in a cardboard box, and she was embarrassed that it was close to Christmas and she had no Santa Claus to send along with him. When she got his father settled in a sanatorium, she said, hugging herself against the cold wind with skinny arms, she would send money for the little boy's keep.

My mother scoffed. Feeding a three-year-old child was no problem. We had plenty, and he was more than welcome. And when she could come, his mother would be welcome, too.

Terry was the delight of our lives. I took him everywhere with me, teaching him rhymes and songs and reading him to sleep at night. My father adored him and rode him around the sawmill and turpentine still on his shoulders. My mother poured fresh milk from our Jersey cow into his thin, blue-john-colored little body and concocted nourishing puddings for him.

She had been right to say we had plenty. Plenty to eat and a roof over our heads, wood for the fire and cover for the beds. A lot of people didn't have it so good.

But money was scarce and Christmas *was* coming. I was of an age where a pair of green corduroy lounging pajamas, homemade, and a box of dusting powder were totally glamorous. But little boys yearned for toys and, looking around, my mother found that even a small red wagon might come as high as five dollars, and toy trains were, of course, for rich children.

It was then that she talked to old Hanse, the wheelwright at the mill. Could he make a little wagon that would do? She knew it wouldn't be a splendid red wagon like the ones McGowin-Lyons Hardware was showing in the window, with rubber-tired wheels and tiny Klaxon horns. But maybe it would do. Could he make it?

Hanse was old and crippled from leg injuries suffered when he was a ship's carpenter on a boat that was swept ashore and shattered in a September storm. He lived alone and worked alone and was brusque and shut-mouthed when interrupted. Worried about Terry's Christmas, my mother interrupted him.

❦ ❦ ❦

He might make the wagon if he had time, he told her. Or he might not. She haunted the carpentry shop, sneaking in when Hanse had quit for the day, feeding her hopes for the wagon on hickory shavings she found beneath his work bench.

In the meantime, she tailored Terry a little wool suit for Sunday school and bought him a cap to go with it, another part of the Christmas present.

Hanse did make the wagon — a plain little wooden vehicle, boxlike and unornamented. But it was sturdy and sanded to a satiny sheen, and its wooden wheels rolled smoothly and silently. That was about the most that could be said for it.

Hanse smiled when he delivered it, coming up the hill at nightfall on his crutches. My mother thanked him and offered him supper and got down her purse to pay him.

He wouldn't take pay, he said. It was the first time he had anything to do with toys or Santa Claus since fifty years ago back in Sweden. He didn't want pay.

I could tell by my mother's face that she wished for the red store-bought wagon instead but she said nothing. And on Christmas morning, Terry was jubilant. It was the grandest toy he could have imagined.

He pulled it over the yard for years, hauling dirt and puppies and stove wood in it — until he outgrew it and went back to live with his parents.

A few years ago, I saw Terry. He had retired from the Navy and moved back to Florida, and he pulled out his wallet to show me a picture. It was the little homemade wagon, filled with holly by his wife for their Christmas table.

December 25, 1988

Weather

$\mathcal{P}$eople who think they can be choosy about the weather really baffle me. The other day we had one of those days of spectacularly uncomfortable weather. At the bus stop my fellow travelers moaned piteously that they had come out without gear adequate to turn the wind and the rain and cushion them against the knife thrusts of the cold. All day long I heard it: "This is a day to stay indoors and read a book." "Not a fit day for *anything*!" "Do you think we'll *ever* see spring?" "Isn't this awful?"

Well, I'm not Pollyanna enough to claim it was balmy or that I luxuriated in soppy feet and buckets full of ice water pouring down my collar. But the alternatives always strike me. Suppose you couldn't get out in it? Suppose you were in jail or sick in bed or dead?

Many times I have written about a man I used to know who was under life sentence for murder and the first thing he noticed when he got out on parole was the feel of the rain on his head and shoulders. When you are in there, he said, nodding toward the jail, you forget what rain feels like.

Then there was the old sea captain whose dilapidated old ship used to ply between the Gulf coastal ports. Storm warnings never stopped him or his craft. A storm eventually did, I'm sorry to say. All hands went down off the coast of Florida. The old man was in his eighties then and he had never found weather a deterrent to anything he wanted to do. His philosophy, oft spoken and not irreverent, I'm sure, was "God makes the weather and I make the trips."

Well, I feel exactly the same. There isn't one thing I can do about the weather and I sure would hate to think it had complete control over my comings and goings. You can be stopped by an icy driveway or skiddy roads, washed out bridges and fallen trees. But that's if you need to travel in a car. As long as you're on foot you're as free as a bird. You can bundle up and slog through the rain and sleet and find, if you seek it stubbornly enough, pleasure in being abroad in the land. The other day I caught the MARTA train to Decatur and delighted anew in that old sense of fellowship, that we're-in-this-together spirit which seems to take hold of people when conditions are adverse. Bus drivers picking up their passengers at the train terminal seemed jollier than usual and took particular care to answer the questions of shivering, rain-drenched people. We talked to one another, smiling and exchanging bits of weather lore, those of us on the train and those of us waiting outside. On an ordinary day when the weather was less notable we would have been silent.

A covey of small children who had evidently embarked on some sightseeing expedition and had to call it on account of the weather, settled happily for a ride on the MARTA train. They loved every sodden, dismal looking view our town had to offer, pointing things out to one another with chirrupy sounds of pleasure. "Lookayonder!" yelled one little boy. "Ain't that a sight?"

And all of us on the train, young and old, craned our necks and looked. We saw nothing but mostly slummy looking dwellings and the gray sky beyond, a picture further dimmed by sleet. But we all grinned and nodded at the little fellow, catching some of his pleasure.

Spring can't come too soon to suit me but if it's held up somewhere I don't mind. I'm not picky about the weather.

March 17, 1980

*I*t isn't a country exclusive, weather, but sometimes it seems to me city dwellers never have it so interesting or abundant as we rural types. Take the thunderstorm that sizzled and roared over Sweet Apple the other afternoon. If I had lived in my old house on 13th Street I might have missed it all. If you have a sound city house with a good roof, air-conditioning and a television set or a lamp to read by, why would you get involved with a thunderstorm?

In the country, you are involved whether you like it or not—and it's pretty wonderful.

The storm came up late toward the shank end of a very hot day. I waited until the flower bed, which we had just cleared of the world's most virulent stand of *vinca major,* was in the shade before I went out to work in it. There were a few odds and ends of plants I had started in the house begging to be set out, and I hacked a place for them at one end of the bed. (Marguerites, something called "candy lilies," do you know them?) By sunset I had progressed, traveling on my knees, of course, to the shade of the hackberry tree where I planned to set out some impatiens. I had about half of them in the ground, set in cow manure and well-watered, when the woods back of the house seemed to come to life.

There were first subdued rumbles and quiet booms. Storm brewing, I thought, and dug on. Suddenly lightning joined in, making the thunder sound like artillery fire, slashing the twilight with brilliant flashes, knifing the sky to empty it of a drenching rain. A little rain wouldn't have driven me in the house but this rain was fierce and hard and cold and there was that lightning, crackling menacingly. So I slogged in the house and washed some of the mud off my hands and knees, deferring the shower until the storm ended, having a perhaps ill-founded notion that lightning strikes people in water more often than dirty-kneed, dirty-footed gardeners on the back porch.

It was just as well because I wasn't half through with the mud when there was a crack somewhere overhead and then an unearthly stillness. Even the rain stopped, as if holding its breath. The electricity, which hums and rumbles an accompaniment to our days and nights, had quit. There was no light, no television, no air-conditioning and, of course, no water, except what happened to be in the tea kettle, enough for a little more cleaning.

We called the power company and then wandered out in the yard to wait. The well-watered earth, which had been dry and crusty earlier, was lush and soft and fragrant. The single white delphinium to bloom this year was heavy with dampness and incredibly beautiful. The lamb's ears held crystal drops of water on their silver gray leaves.

At the edge of the yard the utility pole, which normally holds two wires, held one. Its broken mate trailed impotently through the old crape myrtle trees and on down the road through poison ivy and rampant honeysuckle. Back to call the power men and then to a damp chair on the terrace to wait.

The maple tree by the well house stirred and dripped with a whispery sound. The clouds parted and a bright gold moon rode in a deep blue sky. Back in the woods a whippoorwill sounded and down on the paved road we heard the huffing and puffing of the power company's big trouble truck.

It took the crew an hour or two to find and repair the damaged wires and transformer. I went in the house to look for matches and light candles and kerosene lamps. The little cabin never looks so well as when candle-lit and I pulled up a rocker and admired it and the sweet damp night smells which drifted in through the open windows.

June 2, 1982

*T*he weather has brought disaster to many, many farmers, as well as considerable discomfort to the rest of us. Crops have been wiped out. Peanuts and peas parch in the fields. Even the fruit crops that survived last spring's late freezes are suffering. And yet I keep being amazed that Mother Nature, left to her own devices, somehow seems to muddle through.

By rights my little portion of country should be taking on the aspect of the dust bowl. It is dusty and wilted, the streams are depleted, the little ponds are drying in from the edges. And yet, miraculously enough, it seems to hold on.

The mornings must be the Earth's best time for dew and the night's blessed surcease from the burning sun revive it a little. Still, when I walk in the morning I grieve for the young dogwoods with their drooping leaves. The big ones with old roots going deeper into the Earth seem to bear up better. Such yard plants as have held on in fence rows and around old house sites suffer, yellowing and dropping their leaves. But the wildings manage. Sassafras is lush and green. The young poplars have no more bright yellow leaves than is customary for this time of year. The hickories and pines as good as tell you that the situation is normal.

The wonder is that the battered and weary old Earth knows how to survive. As I climb the hill from the creek I am amazed that the usual late-summer signals are flying. Most flowers are yellow and purple now, fall's colors, but summer's faithful Queen Anne's lace makes a last grab at life, offering a daintier, smaller-sized bouquet than at its prime. And all along the ditch the delicate little My Lady's Bedstraw lifts its tiny white blossoms. (This plant is a good keeper in a vase of water and if you forget to put is in water you will find its dried stems and leaves have a gentle fragrance. It is the plant, according to legend, that Mary used to line the manger to make a soft bed for the Baby Jesus.)

Near the top of the hill but still in the shade of pines and poplars which grow close to the road I am waylaid by a sweet scent I hadn't noticed before. The Earth smells of dust, it's true, but there's something else, a fragrance like orange blossoms or lemons. Could it be the evening primrose, which is said to be lemony smelling? The old field is full of them, still open although their petals will fold fast now that the sun is up. I can't really pinpoint the scent because the field also smells of hay drying and fallen crabapples and something else . . . muscadines ripening! You have to look close to see them. The crop is going to be small this year but among the little clusters of green grapes looped and twirled into the fence wire, there are three dark purple ones. I can't believe my luck.

With muscadines hanging in there, there's hope that persimmons will make it too. I search the trees for what Euell Gibbons called sugar plums. Persimmon trees have to be the least attractive the Earth has to offer — smallish with flabby leaves that freckle early and then attract tent caterpillars. But the fruit smells and tastes of fall. And if you can avoid eating your harvest on the way home it's possible to make some absolutely wonderful persimmon bread. Taking ripe persimmons home is a tricky business, of course. You can't put them in your pocket. They turn to mush. And who remembers to bring a basket or a bag on a hot August morning?

The truth is that we all underestimate nature. I didn't actually find any persimmons. They may not have survived record cold and heat at either end of their growing season. But I wouldn't be surprised if they are around. Old Ma Nature is both more durable and more faithful than we know.

August 31, 1983

*A*longtime weather-watcher and nearly total fan of what they sometimes refer to as "meterological conditions," I recently amazed myself by whining about the neap tide which immobilizes boats at my favorite island. We had an appointment to cross the sound to pick up a couple of relatives of our friends, the Grangers. The only deterrent to meeting them at the ferry dock at 11 A.M. might be the tide. It was possible that the little boat would be sand-locked.

To make sure it was free, we went out in the dark and windy night to move it farther out into the sound. But, as on many nautical matters, we misjudged and anchored that small craft on what was the highest point beneath that pale green water. To my astonishment, when I wandered out to look at the world with my first cup of coffee at sunrise, there sat the boat, high and dry on a kind of sandy hillock. The sand flats extended for what appeared to be miles in each direction and I remembered what we called the "nip" tides of my childhood, when the sun and moon collaborate to pull all of the water out of the bay.

There would be no crossing the big sea water for many hours, and for a while there, I found myself irritated to be frustrated by nature. When my friend Cay arrived, she stood looking at the acres of sand with an occasional tidal pool reflecting the pearl gray sky and long-legged sea birds fishing in them.

"Ah, the beautiful flats," she said. "A good time to go shelling."

We didn't do any shelling beyond picking up an occasional sand dollar to add to the children's motley collection on the back steps. But I suddenly felt consoled about the neap tide and the way nature had taken charge of my day.

It's pretty wonderful that there's one force in our lives for which we have no responsibility and which we can by no dint of technological expertise control. Oh, I know that air conditioning and central heat, man-made weather copers, function and are wonderful. But in larger matters of rain and snow and wind and sleet, of flood and drought and gentle warming sunshine, there isn't a blessed thing we can do.

Somehow, that's cheering. Like children who cry out for discipline and order in their lives, I think the human spirit cries out for control beyond puny human control. Otherwise, how would we know how magnificently powerful weather is.

❦ ❦ ❦

One of the books I was reading at the beach pointed that up abundantly. I've been on a sort of World War II kick lately. I love *Is Paris Burning?* long since read and forgotten by most people, and was delighted to find Cornelius Ryan's account of the June 6, 1944, D-Day invasion of Normandy at a yard sale. Called *The Longest Day* and since seen on television by nearly everybody else, it was to me a fresh and terrible and stunningly moving story.

The enormous importance of the weather, the difference it would make in the entire civilized world, left me breathless with wonder. June is not everywhere the gentle benign month that we know, and that June 1944 was capricious and perilous for the Allied forces that waited in English seaports to cross the channel and drive the Germans out of France. Every movement of the staggering armada, of tanks and guns and men, depended on the weather, and General Dwight Eisenhower spent a lot of time standing outside his trailer looking at the sky, a profoundly human gesture we all know. Fortunately, his corps of meteorologists, who forecast a 24-hour period when the Allied forces could move, differed from Hitler's weathermen, who didn't see it that way. In the midst of horror at the carnage, I couldn't help being glad that even the experts couldn't rubber-stamp the weather.

November 16, 1987